Faith Food

daily devotions for SPRING

Kenneth E. Hagin

Second Edition
Seventh Printing 1995

ISBN 0-89276-042-7

In the U.S. write:
Kenneth Hagin Ministries
P.O. Box 50126
'ulsa, Oklahoma 74150-0126

In Canada write
Kenneth Hagin Ministries
P.O. Box 335, Station D,
Etobicoke, Ontario, M9A 4X3

D0818338

Cover photo by Elwood Chess

Preface

Feed your faith daily! It is of utmost importance to your walk with the Lord. I've written these bite-size pieces of "faith food" to aid you in making sure your faith is fed daily.

F. F. Bosworth said, "Most Christians feed their bodies three hot meals a day, their spirits one cold snack a week, and then they wonder why they are so weak in faith."

Say the confessions found on the bottom of each page aloud. Close your eyes and repeat them. They are based on God's Word. When you hear yourself say these confessions, they will register on your spirit. And when God's Word gets down into your spirit, it will control your life!

Kenneth E. Hagin

About the Author

The ministry of Kenneth E. Hagin has spanned more than 50 years since God miraculously healed him of a deformed heart and incurable blood disease at the age of 17. Today the scope of Kenneth Hagin Ministries is worldwide. The ministry's radio program, "Faith Seminar of the Air," is heard coast-to-coast in the U.S., and reaches more than 80 nations. Other outreaches include: *The Word of Faith,* a free monthly magazine; All Faiths' Crusades, conducted nationwide; RHEMA Correspondence Bible School; RHEMA Bible Training Center; RHEMA Alumni Association and RHEMA Ministerial Association International; and a prison ministry outreach.

By Thy Words

For by thy words thou shalt be justified, and by thy words thou shalt be condemned. — MATTHEW 12:37

Jesus Himself made the above statement.

Words are much more important than many people realize.

Do you remember Job — and those three so-called "friends" who came to comfort Job? Job's cry to those who came as comforters and stayed as tormentors was, *"How long will ye vex my soul, AND BREAK ME IN PIECES WITH WORDS?"* (Job 19:2).

Words make us, or break us.

Words heal us, or make us sick.

According to the teaching of the Bible, words destroy us, or words make us full of life, happy, and healthy.

Words that we spoke yesterday make life what it is today.

That agrees with what Jesus said in Mark 11:23, *". . . he shall have whatsoever he SAITH."*

Those things which you say are words. In fact, you could read that last phrase like this: *". . . he shall have the words that he speaks."*

Confession: *By my words I shall be justified. I know that I shall have whatsoever I say. I shall have the words that I speak. Therefore, I speak words full of life, happiness, and health. I speak words that make, rather than break!*

Power of Life

Death and life are in the power of the tongue: and they that love it shall eat the fruit thereof.

— PROVERBS 18:21

"No, I won't pray for your son," I told the startled widowed mother of a 15-year-old boy. "It won't do any good. As long as you keep telling your son he'll never amount to anything, you'll undo the praying."

"Did the Lord reveal that to you?" she asked.

"No," I said. "I just know that the condition in life that we or our children are in was created by *words.*"

"What shall I do?" she said.

"There are some things you should have done when your son was younger, but he's 15 now. So first, quit nagging him about being saved. Second, instead of lying in bed at night worrying about him, say, 'Lord, I don't know where he is, but wherever he is, I surround him with faith and love.' You've been surrounding him with doubt, fear, and condemnation. Say, 'Lord, I'm going to tell you what I believe. I don't believe he'll end up in the penitentiary. I'll never tell him again he won't amount to anything. I believe he will amount to something.' "

I was back in this woman's city fifteen months later. To make a long story short, she came to me and shared, "It was hard, but I did just what you told me. Before, my son was all out for the devil — but now he's all out for God!"

Confession: *Life is in the power of my tongue, and I will minister life with it. I speak words of life!*

Well of Life

The mouth of a righteous man is a well of life....
— PROVERBS 10:11

Immediately after the births of our son and daughter, I took those little ones into my hands and said, "Lord, I thank You for this child. Because I know the Bible, I realize it is my responsibility to train up this child in the way it should go, and when it is old, it will not depart from it.

"I realize your Word says to bring our children up in the nurture and admonition of the Lord, and I'm going to do that. I know that children are taught in two ways: By precept and by example. So I'm going to live right in front of this child. I will set the right example. Then, too, I know that you can have what you say, so I say over this child that it will grow up strong physically, without sickness and without disease; it will be alert mentally; and stalwart spiritually."

Our children grew up without sickness and disease. I never prayed a prayer that they would be saved. I never prayed a prayer that they would be filled with the Holy Spirit. But both were saved and filled with the Holy Spirit at an early age.

Children are a product of words!

Confession: *According to the New Testament, in Christ I am righteous. Therefore, my mouth is a well of life. I speak words of life concerning others as well as myself!*

Pleasant Words

Pleasant words are as an honeycomb, sweet to the soul, and health to the bones.

— PROVERBS 16:24

Words bless, or words curse.

Words heal, or words make us sick.

Words that we hear in the morning will linger with us throughout the day. Wives and husbands need to realize that a biting, stinging word in the morning will rob their companion of efficiency the whole day long. But a loving, tender, beautiful word, a little prayer word, will fill that loved one with music and lead them into victory.

Parents and children need to realize that the home atmosphere is a product of words.

Learn to make words work for you. Learn to fill words with power that cannot be resisted. How do you do that? By filling your words with faith and love.

Confession: *My words work for me. I fill them with a power that cannot be resisted. I fill my words with faith and love. My words bless. My words heal. My words lead my loved ones into victory. My words charge the atmosphere of my home with faith and love!*

Atmosphere

In the lips of him that hath understanding wisdom is found. . . . Through wisdom is an house builded; and by understanding it is established: And by knowledge shall the chambers be filled with all precious and pleasant riches.
— PROVERBS 10:13; 24:3,4

Spiritual things are created by words. Even natural, physical things are created by words! God, who is a Spirit, said, "Let there be an earth," and there was an earth. Jesus said, ". . . *whosoever shall SAY . . . shall have whatsoever he SAITH*" (Mark 11:23). Atmospheres are created with words.

For example, if you go into a room where fish has been fried, the fish smell is still in the atmosphere. And if you go into a room where harsh words have been spoken, they, too, linger in the atmosphere. The air is heavy with words.

Children brought up in an atmosphere of wrong words become warped. They fail in life, because right words were not spoken to them.

Why is it that some children grow up strong and go out in life's fight and win? It's because the right kinds of words were spoken in their home! Words make children love an education. Words bring children to church.

Confession: *I create the very atmosphere around me with my words. I speak words of wisdom — God's words. I speak words of faith — God's words. I speak words of love — God's words. And the chambers round about me are filled with precious and pleasant riches!*

Wrong Words

Whoso keepeth his mouth and his tongue keepeth his soul from troubles.
— PROVERBS 21:23

When trouble comes, most people want to blame it on God. "Why did God let this happen?" they ask.

After Job's troubles came, he said, *"For the thing which I greatly feared is come upon me, and that which I was afraid of is come unto me"* (Job 3:25). Job opened the door and let the devil in!

We cause our troubles ourselves much of the time. Many dear Christian people don't keep their mouths and tongues under control. They're always saying wrong words. Just about all they ever talk about is what a battle they've had with the devil. Words of defeat are wrong. Words of failure are wrong. Words about how the devil is hindering you, how he's keeping you from success, how he's making you sick and keeping you sick are wrong. Such words give Satan dominion over you and create troubles.

But when you have God's Word in your heart, and speak it out of your mouth, right in the face of apparent contradictions, right in the face of pain, right in the face of alarming symptoms, right in the face of excruciating circumstances, such adverse conditions will disappear.

Confession: *I keep my mouth, and I keep my tongue. Therefore, I keep my soul from troubles. I believe God's Word in my heart. I purpose that the Word shall be in my mouth and on my tongue — and that I shall only speak according to God's Word!*

Health Words

There is that speaketh like the piercings of a sword: but the tongue of the wise is health.

— PROVERBS 12:18

I first learned the secret of words — faith words — on the bed of sickness, where I spent sixteen months, given up to die by five doctors.

But one August day in 1934, as I lay in that bed, I acted on Mark 11:23,24, and I *said! Words* were spoken!

I *said,* "I believe that I receive healing for the deformed heart. I believe that I receive healing for the incurable blood disease. I believe that I receive healing for the paralysis. I believe that I receive healing from the top of my head to the soles of my feet." Within the hour, I was standing on my feet beside the bed — healed!

Now more than 50 years have come and gone, and I haven't even had a headache. And I won't have one. But if I did have one — which I haven't — I wouldn't say my head hurt. Why? Because Jesus said, "... *he shall have whatsoever he saith.*" If someone were to ask me in such a case, "How are you feeling?" I'd reply, "I'm fine, thank you. You see, the Word of God says that by His stripes I am healed. So I believe that I am healed. And the Word of God says ... " And I would speak the right words — for the tongue of the wise is health!

Confession: *My tongue is health. It speaks words of life and health. I talk health. Therefore, I walk in health.*

Transformed Talk

Blessed is the man that walketh not in the counsel of the ungodly. . . .
— PSALM 1:1

. . . be not conformed to this world: but be ye transformed by the renewing of your mind. . . .
— ROMANS 12:2

When God's Word tells us not to be conformed to this world, notice that it relates conformity to the area of the mind. In other words, we are told not to think like the world thinks; we are to get our mind *renewed* with the Word of God and *think* in line with the Word of God. Then we will *talk* and *believe* in line with the Word of God.

The world is programmed negatively. The world thinks sickness, fear, doubt, defeat, and failure. That's because the world without God is in spiritual death. It is therefore programmed to death instead of to life. Listen to what people say: "That scares me to death."

If Christians do not renew their minds with the Word of God, they will make the same mistake the world makes. They'll talk themselves into sickness. But if we'll renew our mind with the Word of God, we'll know that God says, ". . . *the tongue of the wise is health.*"

Confession: *I never talk sickness. I don't believe in sickness. I talk health. The tongue of the wise is health. I believe in healing and health. I never talk failure. I don't believe in failure. I believe in success. I never talk doubt. I refuse to doubt. I never talk defeat. I don't believe in defeat. I never talk about what the devil is doing. I talk about the works of God.*

Overcoming Faith

For whatsoever is born of God overcometh the world: and this is the victory that overcometh the world, even our faith.
— 1 JOHN 5:4

I may be in the world, but I am not of the world. I am of God. My citizenship is in heaven. And while I am in this world, I have the Greater One living in me. Greater is He that is in me, than he that is in the world (1 John 4:4).

Who is in the world? The devil. He's called the god of this world in Second Corinthians 4:4.

What is in the world? Sin. But the Greater One in me is greater than sin. The Greater One conquered sin.

What else is in the world? Sickness. It's not of God. It doesn't come from heaven. There's no sickness up there. Sickness is of this world. But the Greater One in me is the Healer.

What else is in the world? Trouble. Adverse circumstances. Seeming impossibilities. But when I've faced such things, I've just remembered who is on the inside of me and what the Bible says. I didn't even have to pray about it. I just looked that circumstance right in the face and laughed as I said, "If I don't make it *over* you, I'll make it *around* you. If I don't make it *around* you, I'll make it *under* you. If I don't make it *under* you, I'll make it *through* you, because the Greater One is in me!" Even while I laughed, that circumstance ran off and hid!

Confession: *I am born of God. And by releasing my faith in words through my mouth, I overcome the world!*

9

Fruit of the Mouth

A man's belly shall be satisfied with the fruit of his mouth; and with the increase of his lips shall he be filled.

— PROVERBS 18:20

You won't get the blessings of God just because you believe.

You don't get saved, healed, or get answers to prayer just because you believe.

Most Christians think that is the case, but the Bible doesn't teach that. The Bible teaches that you must *believe and you must say* something.

For example, in order to be saved, Romans 10:9,10 says, *"That if thou shalt CONFESS WITH THY MOUTH the Lord Jesus, and shalt believe in thine heart that God hath raised him from the dead, thou shalt be saved."* Notice it doesn't say you'll be saved just because you believe. The very next verse says, *"For with the heart man believeth unto righteousness; AND WITH THE MOUTH CONFESSION IS MADE UNTO SALVATION."*

Jesus didn't conclude Mark 11:23 by saying you'd have whatsoever you believed. He concluded it by saying, *" . . . he shall have whatsoever he SAITH."*

Faith is always expressed in WORDS! The words that you speak — not just on Sunday, in church, or when you pray, but the words you speak in your everyday life, at home, with your friends, and on your job — determine what you have in life.

Confession: *I purpose that I shall speak only according to God's Word!*

Saying the Same Thing

Seeing then that we have a great high priest, that is passed into the heavens, Jesus the Son of God, let us hold fast our profession [confession].

— HEBREWS 4:14

The Greek word translated "profession" here is translated "confession" elsewhere in the *King James Version*. The literal Greek meaning of this word is "to speak the same thing." So instead of saying, "Let us hold fast our confession," we could say, "Let us hold fast to speaking the same thing." Notice that *words* are involved here.

The thing that defeats many people is that they have a double confession. One time they confess one thing, and the next time, something else.

For example, they may say to you, "Yes, the Lord is my Shepherd, and I shall not want. According to Philippians 4:19, my God shall supply all my need according to His riches in glory by Christ Jesus — and I'm believing God to supply my needs."

But when they leave you and meet somebody else, their mind may revert back to their problems, so they'll say, "We're not doing so good. We can't pay our phone bill. We're going to have to take the phone out. And it even looks like we're going to lose our car . . . "

What about that first confession they made? It was nullified by the second!

Confession: *I make my mouth do its duty. I see to it that I speak in line with God's Word. Then I hold fast to my confession!*

A Psalm

Let the word of Christ dwell in you richly in all wisdom;
teaching and admonishing one another in psalms and
hymns and spiritual songs....

— COLOSSIANS 3:16

Here is a psalm the Holy Spirit gave me on the
subject of words.

Words seem so insignificant and small
that men oft times take no note of them at all.
But words spoken in faith, create realities . . .
So rise up and speak, like the Creator of the universe,
Who, in faith, said, LET THERE BE —
and THERE WAS.

Words — you speak them all the time,
filled with negativism and defeat,
Those words create defeat, and make you
unsuccessful, unhealthy, and unwise.

But Words given by God, inspired by His Spirit,
called by men, the Holy Writ,
These words heard with the ear of faith,
And spoken out of a heart filled with faith,
Will create in your life, and your family's too,
Success and victory; health and healing;
Circumstances and darkness and troubles too,
will run away from you.

Filled with His Word, inspired by His Spirit,
Make your tongue do its duty.
See to it that you speak only truth . . .
His Word is truth.
Speak words of faith and love; words that are true,
And no longer will spiritual realities unto you,
seem unreal and far away.
But all of the blessings of life;
spiritual, material, physical, and financial too,
Will come to make their abode with you.

God's Medicine

My son, attend to my words; incline thine ear unto my sayings. Let them not depart from thine eyes; keep them in the midst of thine heart. For they are life unto those that find them, and health [medicine] *to all their flesh.*

— PROVERBS 4:20-22

A marginal note in a good reference Bible will show that the last phrase of the above text can read "and medicine to all their flesh." *This means that God has "prescribed" His Words for our healing and for our health!*

But medicine, even in the natural, won't do any good unless you take it according to directions. You could go to a doctor, get a prescription, have it filled, take it home, set it on your bedside table — and still grow steadily worse! You could call the doctor and complain, "I don't understand it. I paid good money for this prescription, but I'm getting worse." The doctor might ask, "Are you taking your medicine according to the directions?" "Well, no, but I've got it right here in the bottle at my bedside." The medicine won't work just because it's in the bottle. You've got to get it *in you!*

And God's medicine (your Bible) won't work just because you have it on your bedside table. But it will work if you'll get it down on the inside of you — into your heart, or spirit. And not just by reading it and forgetting it; but by meditating upon it until it becomes a part of your inward man.

Confession: *I hide God's Words in the midst of my heart. They are life to me. They are medicine to my flesh!*

Obstacles

... and much people followed him [Jesus], *and thronged him. And a certain woman, which had an issue of blood twelve years. . . . When she had heard of Jesus, came in the press behind, and touched his garment.*

— MARK 5:24,25,27

To receive her healing, this woman had a number of obstacles to overcome. In her religious tradition, a woman with an issue of blood was considered in the same category as a leper. She was not supposed to mingle in public. If anyone came close to her, she was to cry, "Unclean! Unclean!" In fact, the women in ancient Israel didn't have the same rights and privileges to mix freely in public that most women in the modern world have.

You could say that a multitude of people stood between this woman and her healing. Public sentiment and her own religious teachings stood between her and getting to Jesus. But she overcame all obstacles. She got into the very midst of the crowd, and she reached through to touch Jesus' clothes.

This woman didn't pray that God would overcome the obstacles; she did something about them herself! You, too, will have to do something yourself about the obstacles that confront you. Too many people expect God to do everything, leaving no part for them to play in receiving His blessings. But we do have a part to play. Receiving from God is a faith proposition.

Confession: *I am a believer. I am not a doubter. I have faith. I am an overcomer. No obstacle to the blessings of God can stand in my way. I overcome all obstacles by faith in God's Word!*

Step 1: Say It

For she said, If I may touch but his clothes, I shall be whole.
And straightway the fountain of her blood was dried up. . . .
And he [Jesus] said unto her, Daughter, thy faith hath made
thee whole. . . . — MARK 5:28,29,34

In 1953, during a vision, the Lord Jesus Christ gave me a sermon. He told me to get pencil and paper and to write down 1,2,3,4. Then He said, "If anybody, anywhere, will take these four steps, or put these four principles into operation, they will always receive whatever they want from Me, or from God the Father."

The steps Jesus gave are simple. They are: (1) *Say it;* (2) *Do it;* (3) *Receive it;* and (4) *Tell it.* Jesus used the healing of the woman with the issue of blood to illustrate these four steps.

Step 1: Say It. What was the woman's first step toward being healed? "For she said. . . ." Jesus told me, "Positive or negative, according to what the individual says, that shall he receive. This woman could have made a negative statement instead of a positive one. She could have said, 'There's no use. I've suffered so long. All the best doctors have given up on my case. I might as well go ahead and die' — and that would have been what she received. But she made a positive statement — and it came to pass."

What this woman said was her faith speaking.

Confession: *I have what I say. I speak positively — and I receive accordingly. What I say is my faith speaking. And what I say makes me whole.*

Step 2: Do It

What good is it, my brethren, if a man professes to have faith, and yet his actions do not correspond . . . . some one will say, "You have faith, I have actions: prove to me your faith apart from corresponding actions and I will prove mine to you by my actions. . . ." You notice that his [Abraham's] faith was co-operating with his actions, and that by his actions his faith was perfected.

— JAMES 2:14,18,22 *Weymouth*

Step 2: Do It. It wouldn't have done that woman with the issue of blood any good to have said, "If I may but touch His clothes I shall be whole," if she hadn't *acted* on what she said.

Jesus said to me in that vision, "Your actions defeat you, or they put you over. According to your actions, you receive, or you are kept from receiving."

That's important. Read it again.

The Book of James is written to *believers.* James said, "What doth it profit, *my brethren. . . .*" Most people think James was writing about salvation, but he was writing to people who are already saved, pointing out that faith without corresponding actions won't work. It is a great mistake to confess faith in the Word of God and, at the same time, contradict your confession by wrong actions. Actions must correspond with your saying and believing in order to receive from God.

This woman said, "If I may touch but His clothes, I shall be whole," and then she acted on that — and she received!

Confession: *My actions line up with God's Word. My actions put me over. By my actions I receive from God!*

Step 3: Receive It

And straightway the fountain of her blood was dried up; and she felt in her body that she was healed of that plague. And Jesus, immediately knowing in himself that virtue [power] had gone out of him, turned him about in the press, and said, Who touched my clothes?

— MARK 5:29,30

Jesus knew that *power* had gone out of Him. At that time, Jesus was the only representative of the Godhead at work upon the earth. He was anointed with the Holy Spirit (Acts 10:38). In that day, to get to where the power was, you had to go to where Jesus was. Today, the Holy Spirit is the Person of the Godhead who is at work upon the earth. He is everywhere present — and wherever the Holy Spirit is, there is *power.*

Nuclear bombs release radioactivity into the atmosphere — a power that can neither be seen or felt, but a power that is both dangerous and deadly. However, there is a power working upon the earth this moment that is neither dangerous nor deadly; a power that is good, that heals, and that sets men free — the power of the Holy Spirit!

Jesus said to me when He gave me these four steps, "Power is always present everywhere. Faith gives it action, or puts it to work, or uses it."

This woman's faith caused the power to flow from Jesus into her. With our faith, we can plug into the power of God that is everywhere present, and we can put that power to work for us!

Confession: *I recognize that God's power is everywhere present. And I know how to plug into that power and put it to work for me. Faith is the plug.*

Step 4: Tell It

O give thanks unto the Lord; call upon his name: make known his deeds among the people. Sing unto him, sing psalms unto him: talk ye of all his wondrous works.

— PSALM 105:1,2

Step 4: Tell it. This woman, "*. . . knowing what was done in her, came and fell down before him, and told him all the truth*" (Mark 5:33). Not only did Jesus hear her, but the whole crowd heard her. Jesus said to me concerning this step, "Tell it so that others may believe it or receive it."

There is a difference between this step and the first step. The first is, Say it. This fourth step is, Tell it.

The woman *said* what she believed. Then, after she received, she *told* what had happened to her.

1. Say it.
2. Do it.
3. Receive it.
4. Tell it.

I asked Jesus, when He gave me these steps, "Are you telling me that any believer, anywhere, can write a ticket of victory over the world, the flesh, and the devil?"

"Emphatically yes," Jesus answered. "And if they don't do it, it won't be done. They'll be wasting their time to pray that I will give them the victory. They'll have to write their own ticket."

Confession: *I give thanks unto the Lord. I make known His deeds among the people. I sing unto Him. I sing psalms unto Him. I talk of all His wondrous works!*

David and Goliath

Then said David to the Philistine, Thou comest to me with a sword, and with a spear, and with a shield: but I come to thee in the name of the Lord of hosts, the God of the armies of Israel, whom thou hast defied. This day will the Lord deliver thee into mine hand; and I will smite thee, and take thine head from thee; and I will give the carcases of the host of the Philistines this day unto the fowls of the air, and to the wild beasts of the earth; that all the earth may know that there is a God in Israel. And all this assembly shall know that the Lord saveth not with sword and spear: for the battle is the Lord's, and he will give you into our hands.   — 1 SAMUEL 17:45-47

I asked the Lord to give me more Scriptures which use these same four principles.

Jesus smiled and said, "All right. They're in an Old Testament story you've known from your youth — the story of David and Goliath."

"Is that what David did?" I asked.

"Exactly," Jesus said. "Those are the four steps David took."

After the vision was over, I reread the story of David and Goliath. I discovered that five times David *said it* before he acted on it! Read it yourself. David knew you can have what you say. He knew you could write your own ticket with God. How did David know God would do it? David knew God would do anything he would believe Him for — and God will do it for you too!

Confession: *I am a believer. I am not a doubter. I believe God for total victory. Then the world will see that God is in me!*

The Prodigal

And when he came to himself, he said, How many hired servants of my father's have bread enough and to spare, and I perish with hunger! I will arise and go to my father, and will say unto him, Father, I have sinned against heaven, and before thee, And am no more worthy to be called thy son: make me as one of thy hired servants. And he arose, and came to his father....
— LUKE 15:17-20

Jesus gave me this example from the New Testament of these four principles being followed.

Notice that the first thing the prodigal son did was, *he said it!*

Then, *he did it.* He climbed out of that hog pasture, and he started down the road toward home.

Next, *he received it.* His father saw him coming afar off, and had compassion, and ran, and fell on his neck, and kissed him. His father said, "Bring the robe and put it on him. Bring the ring and put it on his finger. Bring shoes and put them on his feet. Kill the fatted calf."

Then they had a celebration and *told it.*

Confession: *I know that God will do anything I believe Him to do which is in line with His Word. And I know how to write my own ticket with God. First, I say it. Next, I do it. Next, I receive it. Finally, I tell it!*

Wisdom and Revelation

[I] *Cease not to give thanks for you, making mention of you in my prayers.* — EPHESIANS 1:16

Ephesians 1:17-23 and 3:14-21 are Holy Spirit-given prayers which apply to the Church everywhere. The turning point in my life came when I prayed them a thousand times or more for myself. I would kneel, open my Bible, and say, "Father, I'm praying these prayers for myself. Because they are Spirit-given prayers, this has to be your will for me, just as it was your will for the Church at Ephesus." Then I would continue to pray by reading from these passages, except where Paul said "you," I would substitute "me," like this:

That the God of our Lord Jesus Christ, the Father of glory, may give unto "me" the spirit of wisdom and revelation in the knowledge of him:
The eyes of "my" understanding being enlightened; that "I" may know what is the hope of his calling, and what the riches of the glory of his inheritance in the saints, And what is the exceeding greatness of his power to usward who believe, according to the working of his mighty power, Which he wrought in Christ, when he raised him from the dead, and set him at his own right hand in the heavenly places. . . .

After about six months, the first thing I was praying about started to happen: The revelation of God's Word began to come to me!

Confession: *Pray the prayer in Ephesians chapter one for yourself.*

For This Cause

For this cause I bow my knees unto the Father of our Lord
Jesus Christ. . . . — EPHESIANS 3:14

The second prayer I would pray was this one
from the third chapter of Ephesians. And I'd pray
it for myself like this:

> *For this cause I bow my knees unto the Father of our Lord*
> *Jesus Christ,*
> *Of whom the whole family in heaven and earth is named,*
> *That he would grant "me," according to the riches of his*
> *glory, to be strengthened with might by his Spirit in "my"*
> *inner man;*
> *That Christ may dwell in "my" heart by faith; that "I," being*
> *rooted and grounded in love, May be able to comprehend*
> *with all saints what is the breadth, and length, and depth,*
> *and height;*
> *And to know the love of Christ, which passeth knowledge,*
> *that "I" might be filled with all the fulness of God.*
> *Now unto him that is able to do exceeding abundantly above*
> *all that we ask or think, according to the power that*
> *worketh in us,*
> *Unto him be glory in the church by Christ Jesus throughout*
> *all ages, world without end.*

I suggest that you pray these Ephesian prayers
for yourself. Stay at it. It won't work if you pray
them just on a hit-and-miss basis. But if you'll stay
with it, praise God, they will work for you!

Confession: *Pray yesterday's and today's prayers for*
yourself.

For Another

I have no greater joy than to hear that my children walk in truth. — 3 JOHN 4

When a Spirit-filled relative of mine couldn't seem to grasp certain important Bible truths, I prayed the Ephesian prayers for him every morning and night, inserting his name in the appropriate places.

Lord, I'm praying this prayer for "Joe." God of our Lord Jesus Christ, the Father of glory, give unto "Joe" the spirit of wisdom and revelation in the knowledge of Him. I pray that the eyes of "Joe's" understanding be enlightened; that "Joe" may know what is the hope of His calling, and what is the riches of the glory of His inheritance in the saints. . . .

And I continued on through both prayers. I prayed these prayers for him morning and night for ten days. Finally he wrote me, saying, "It's amazing how things have opened up to me. I'm beginning to see what you've been talking about." No human teacher had talked to him about spiritual matters.

People frequently want to know how to pray for friends and loved ones. Some people just pray, "God bless them." But God has *already* blessed them with all spiritual blessings in heavenly places in Christ Jesus (Eph. 1:3). They just don't know it, so they can't take advantage of it. Pray these Ephesian prayers for your friends and loved ones. Stay with it — morning and night, and more frequently if you can.

Confession: *Pray the Ephesian prayers for someone you desire to walk in the truth.*

Authority

Behold, I give unto you power [authority] *to tread on serpents and scorpions, and over all the power of the enemy: and nothing shall by any means hurt you.*

— LUKE 10:19

The Greek word *exousia* means "authority." However, it is often translated as "power" in the *King James Version* of the New Testament. In our text, for example, two different Greek words are translated as "power," yet the correct translation of the first word is "authority." Our verse should read, "I give you *authority* to tread on serpents and scorpions, and over all the *power* of the enemy. . . ."

What is the difference between power and authority?

Well, what can one uniformed police officer do to direct the flow of rush hour traffic? He can do a great deal. Is it because the policeman has the *power* to hold back these mighty machines? No! His most strenuous efforts couldn't stop the swiftly passing cars. He doesn't have the power to do it, but he has something far better. He is invested with the *authority* of the government he serves. Even a stranger in the city recognizes this authority and obeys it.

Authority is delegated power.

Confession: *I have been given authority to tread on serpents and scorpions, and over all the power of the enemy. Nothing shall by any means hurt me.*

Delegated Power

And Jesus came and spake unto them, saying, All power
[authority] *is given unto me in heaven and in earth. Go*
ye therefore.... — MATTHEW 28:18,19

The authority on earth that is invested in the
Name of Jesus Christ and was obtained by Him
through His overcoming Satan was then delegated
by Jesus Christ to the Church.

Jesus spoke these words in Matthew 28 after
His death on the cross, after His burial, after His
defeat of Satan in hell, after His resurrection, after
His ascension with His own blood to the heavenly
Holy of Holies — but just *before* His ascension to
be seated at the right hand of the Father. Jesus
said that all authority in heaven and on earth is
given to Him. Then He immediately transferred
this authority on earth to His Church, saying, "*Go*
ye therefore...."

Mark records that Jesus said at this same time,
"*And these signs shall follow them that believe;*
In my name shall they cast out devils; they shall
speak with new tongues; They shall take up
serpents; and if they drink any deadly thing, it
shall not hurt them; they shall lay hands on the
sick, and they shall recover" (Mark 16:17,18).

Confession: *The authority in the Name that is above every*
name has been given to the Church. It has been given to
me. I have authority over all the power of the enemy.

Be Strong

Finally, my brethren, be strong in the Lord, and in the power of his might. Put on the whole armour of God, that ye may be able to stand against the wiles of the devil.
— EPHESIANS 6:10,11

What would you think if you went downtown and saw a traffic policeman in front of a car, trying to hold it back? You'd think, *He can't do that. He's no match for that car!*

Some people read Ephesians 6:10 and think that the Lord is telling them to be strong in themselves. And they're trying to be strong. They'll say, "Oh, pray for me that I'll hold out faithful to the end!" But God didn't say a word about our being strong in ourselves or in the power of our might.

That traffic policeman steps right out in front of those cars and holds up his hand, because he knows they're going to stop for him. He doesn't have to exert any strength himself; he's strong in the authority that has been given to him.

That is what the Lord is telling us. He's saying. "Be strong in the Lord. Be strong in the authority of His might. Just step out there in front of that oncoming devil. Hold up your hand in the Name of Jesus, and say, 'Thus far, and no farther! Stop right now!' "

Confession: *I am strong in the Lord and in the power of His might. I am invested with authority from the Lord Jesus Christ. When I hold up my hand in the Name of Jesus and say, "Thus far, and no farther," the devil stops in his tracks!*

Whom Resist

Be sober, be vigilant; because your adversary the devil, as a roaring lion, walketh about, seeking whom he may devour: Whom resist stedfast in the faith. . . .

— 1 PETER 5:8,9

In 1942, I had a battle with symptoms in my body. I prayed, appropriated the promises of God, and stood my ground. But at times it looked like I wasn't going to make it.

One such night I had a dream. I dreamed another man and I were on some kind of a parade ground. It was like a football field. There were stands on either side. As we walked along talking, suddenly the man looked back and yelled, "Look!" and he started running. I turned and saw that two ferocious lions were almost upon me. I ran about two steps. Then I hollered to the other man, "You'll never make it. You can't outrun them!" I stopped still, turned around, and faced them. I was trembling. My flesh was covered with goose pimples. But I said, "I stand against you. I refuse to budge in the Name of Jesus Christ." The lions stopped, came right up to me, sniffed around my feet, and just trotted off. I awoke, and First Peter 5:8 came to mind. I knew my physical battle was won. I received healing immediately. I had almost run, but I had stood my ground. I had used my authority.

Confession: *I resist the devil steadfast in the faith. I stand my ground. I use my authority. And the devil runs from me as if in terror.*

Source

Behold, I have given you authority to tread upon serpents and scorpions, and over all the power of the enemy: and nothing shall in any wise hurt you.

— LUKE 10:19 ASV (1901)

Authority is delegated power.

Its value depends on the force behind the user.

Jesus said, "I have given you authority." Who gave it? Jesus did. Who is Jesus? *Jesus is God manifested in the flesh!* That means that God said it. Therefore, God said, "I have given you authority to tread upon serpents and scorpions, and over all the power of the enemy...."

(Serpents and scorpions represent demons and evil spirits and the power of the enemy.)

God Himself is the Power, the Force, behind this authority. The believer who is fully conscious of divine power behind him and of his own authority can therefore face the enemy without fear or hesitation.

Behind the authority possessed by the believer is a Power far greater than the power that backs our enemies. And those enemies are *compelled* to recognize that authority!

No wonder John says, *"... greater is he that is in you than he that is in the world"* (1 John 4:4).

Confession: *I am a believer. Jesus has given me authority. God has given me authority. God Himself is the Power behind this authority. And this authority God has given me is over all the power of the enemy!*

Resurrection Power

That I may know him, and the power of his resurrection. . . .
— PHILIPPIANS 3:10

Paul was actually praying in Ephesians that the Church would receive revelation knowledge of spiritual things. If you've been praying the Ephesian prayers for yourself, as I've suggested, you know that Paul wanted the believers at Ephesus to know:

... the exceeding greatness of his power to usward who believe, according to the working of his mighty power, Which he wrought in Christ, when he raised him from the dead, and set him at his own right hand in the heavenly places, Far above all principality, and power, and might, and dominion, and every name that is named, not only in this world, but also in that which is to come.

— EPHESIANS 1:19-21

There was such a manifestation of the divine omnipotence of God's power in raising Jesus from the dead that it is actually the mightiest working of God! And God wants us to know what happened when this occurred.

The resurrection was opposed by all the tremendous powers of the air. These evil forces endeavored to defeat the plan of God. But these powers were overthrown by our Lord Jesus Christ, and He has been enthroned far above them, ruling with the authority of the Most High. Thus, the source of our authority is found in this resurrection and seating of Christ by God.

Confession: *The Power that raised Jesus from the dead is the Corporation behind my authority!*

To Usward

Many, O Lord my God, are thy wonderful works which thou hast done, and thy thoughts which are to usward. . . .

— PSALM 40:5

Did you notice this phrase in Ephesians 1:19, "*. . . the exceeding greatness of his power to usward who believe. . . .*"?

All the demonstration of the glory of God shown in the manifestation of His omnipotence pointed to man — "to usward."

The cross of Christ — with what it revealed of obedience to God, atonement for sin, and crushing defeat for the enemies of divine authority — shows us a representative Man.

Christ was our Representative, our Substitute — overcoming for mankind and preparing a throne and a heavenly ministry for those who should overcome through Him.

The source of our authority is therefore found in the resurrection and seating of Christ by God. In the Book of Ephesians, we learn that God wants the Church to gain revelation knowledge of all that this means to us.

Confession: *I am a believer. I am receiving the spirit of wisdom and revelation in the knowledge of God. The eyes of my understanding are being enlightened that I may know what is the exceeding greatness of God's power to usward who believe!*

Raised Together

And what is the exceeding greatness of his power.... Which he wrought in Christ, WHEN HE RAISED HIM from the dead, AND SET HIM at his own right hand in the heavenly places.... AND YOU hath he quickened, who were dead in trespasses and sins.

— EPHESIANS 1:19,20; 2:1

Open your own Bible to Ephesians 2:1. A *King James Version* will look something like this:

CHAPTER 2

AND you *hath he quickened,* who were dead in trespasses and sins.

When a word is italicized in the *King James Version,* that means the word is not in the original manuscripts; the translators have added it. So the original reads, "And you who were dead in trespasses and sins."

I wanted you to see that the verb that controls this first verse of chapter two is back in the twentieth verse of chapter one! (Paul didn't write in chapters and verses; men divided Paul's writings later for easy reference.) Our text today makes it clearer for you. Notice the capitalized words: "... *WHEN HE* [God] *RAISED HIM* [Christ] *from the dead .. AND* [raised] *YOU ... who were dead in trespasses and sins.*" The same verb that expresses the reviving of Christ *also* expresses the reviving of Christ's people! So the mighty act of God which raised Christ from the dead also raised His Body!

Confession: *The same mighty Power that raised Jesus from the dead also raised me!*

31

Seated Together

Even when we were dead in sins, [God] *hath quickened us together with Christ, (by grace ye are saved;) And hath raised us up together, and made us sit together in heavenly places in Christ Jesus.* — EPHESIANS 2:5,6

The very act that raised the Lord from the dead also raised His Body. (The head and the body are naturally raised together.)

Furthermore, the very act that seated Christ also seated His Body. Where are we sitting? In heavenly places! Right now! We're not going to sit there *sometime;* God has made us sit together *now* in heavenly places in Christ Jesus.

Christ is seated at the Father's own right hand. Therefore, we are seated at the Father's own right hand! (The right hand is the place of authority. God carries out all of His plan and program through His right hand — through Christ, through His spiritual Body, which is the Church.)

The right hand of the throne of Majesty (Heb. 8:1) in the heavens is the center of power of the whole universe! The exercising of the power of that throne was committed to the ascended Christ — and that authority belongs to us.

Confession: *God has quickened me with Christ. God has raised me up together with Him. God has made me sit together with Christ in heavenly places. As I go about in the earth, working with God in carrying out His plan, I am seated, as far as authority goes, at the Father's right hand.*

Under Our Feet

*... and set him at his own right hand in the heavenly places,
Far above all principality, and power, and might, and
dominion, and every name that is named, not only in this
world, but also in that which is to come: And hath put all
things under his feet, and gave him to be the head over
all things to the church, Which is his body, the fulness of
him that filleth all in all.*

— EPHESIANS 1:20-23

The Church is the Body of the Lord Jesus Christ. We are the Body of Christ.

Now for a question: Where are the feet? Are they in the head, or are they in the body? They're in the body, of course.

Look again at today's text. It describes positionally where we are seated.

God has put all things under Christ's feet. Christ's feet are in His Body. Therefore, all things have been put under *our* feet!

What are the "all things" Paul is talking about? Principalities, powers, might and dominion. In other words, all the power of the enemy is under our feet!

Someone has said that if we have anything to say to Satan, we should write it on the bottoms of our shoes!

Confession: *I am seated with Christ in heavenly places.
I am a member in particular of the Body of Christ. All the
power of the enemy is under my feet!*

Because I Go

Verily, verily, I say unto you, He that believeth on me, the works that I do shall he do also; and greater works than these shall he do; because I go unto my Father.

— JOHN 14:12

Dr. John Alexander Dowie (1847-1907) was used by God to reintroduce divine healing to the modern Church.

Dr. P. C. Nelson, founder of Southwestern Assemblies of God College, said, "You can't follow Dowie's doctrine, but you can follow his faith."

I heard Dr. Nelson tell about how when he himself was a young Baptist minister, he saw Dowie minister to a woman with a purplish-blue cancerous growth that covered most of her face.

Nelson said, "I saw Dowie, in the presence of us six denominational ministers and three medical doctors, just reach out and take hold of that cancer, saying, 'In the Name of the Lord Jesus Christ!' — and then strip it off that woman's face. The doctors present examined her immediately, and said the skin on her face was like the skin of a newborn baby."

The reason Jesus gave, that those who believe on Him would be able to do the works He did was, "*. . . because I go unto my Father.*" It's because of Jesus' seating at the right hand of the Father on High in the place of authority that believers can do these same works.

Confession: *I believe on Jesus. Because Jesus went to His Father and mine, and is seated at the right hand of Majesty on High — and I am seated with Him — I can do the works of my Father, in Jesus' Name.*

The Works That I Do

Now it came to pass on a certain day, that he went into a ship with his disciples: and he said unto them, Let us go over unto the other side of the lake. And they launched forth. But as they sailed he fell asleep: and there came down a storm of wind on the lake; and they were filled with water, and were in jeopardy. And they came to him, and awoke him, saying, Master, master, we perish. Then he arose, and rebuked the wind and the raging of the water: and they ceased, and there was a calm. And he said unto them, Where is your faith? . . . — LUKE 8:22-25

John Alexander Dowie was born in Edinburgh, Scotland, and moved to Australia as a young man. About 1875, while Dowie was pastoring a Congregational church in Newton, Australia, a terrible plague swept through that part of the country. It was during this plague that Dowie first received light on divine healing and the authority that believers possess.

I read that Dowie once said, "I have crossed the ocean fourteen times by ship. During those fourteen crossings, many storms arose. But every time a storm came up, I always did like Jesus did: I rebuked that storm. And every single one ceased."

Dowie knew that Jesus had said, "*He that believeth on me, the works that I do shall he do also. . . .*" Dowie knew that he was linked up with God. You and I are linked up with God just as much as Dowie or anybody else ever was.

Confession: *I believe on Jesus. The works that Jesus did on the earth, I can do. Jesus said I could, so I can.*

Edge of Authority

.. and they awake him, and say unto him, Master, carest thou not that we perish? And he arose, and rebuked the wind, and said unto the sea, Peace, be still. And the wind ceased, and there was a great calm.

— MARK 4:38,39

A great storm — a tornado — arose one spring day down in Texas. Most people had gone into their storm cellars. We didn't have one. I was bedfast and almost totally paralyzed anyway. I became fearful. If the tornado were to strike, it would strike my corner room first, because the wind was coming from that direction. The house would cave in right where I was!

In desperation, and without thinking whether or not I could do it, I said, "Dear Lord, I'm your child. When those disciples were about to sink, they awakened You and said, 'Carest thou not that we perish?' And You did care. You awoke and rebuked the wind. I know You don't want me to perish, but I can't get out of here. I'm here on this bed, and this wall is about to blow in on top of me. So I now rebuke this storm in Jesus' Name!"

As fast as you'd snap your fingers, the storm stopped. It grew calm. I rejoiced. I didn't know then the great truths about the believer's authority. I had gotten to the edge of it and had exercised it without really knowing what I had done. But God wants us to get the revelation of the truth of His Word so we can understand what belongs to us and use it in our lives.

Confession: *I will get the revelation of the truth of God's Word and understand and use what belongs to me.*

Dethroned Powers

We do discuss 'wisdom' with those who are mature; only it is not the wisdom of this world or of the dethroned Powers who rule this world, it is the mysterious Wisdom of God....
— 1 CORINTHIANS 2:6,7 *Moffatt*

God's Word teaches that Satan and evil spirits are rebel holders of authority, and that they have been dethroned by the Lord Jesus Christ. Notice how Moffatt's translation calls them "dethroned Powers who rule this world."

God made the earth and the fullness thereof. Then He gave Adam dominion, or authority, over all the works of His hands (Gen. 1:27,28; Ps. 8:3-6). Adam had dominion on the earth. In fact, Adam was made the god of this world. When he committed high treason and sold out to Satan, then Satan, through Adam, became the god of this world (2 Cor. 4:4), and a rebel holder of Adam's authority.

But the Bible calls Jesus Christ the last Adam (1 Cor. 15:45). Jesus came as our Representative — our Substitute — and defeated Satan! Jesus didn't do it for Himself; He did it for us! *All that Jesus did belongs to us.*

We believers are to remember that we are in the world, but we're not of it. Satan is not to dominate us. We are to dominate Satan. We can dominate Satan. We have authority over him. Jesus defeated him for us.

Confession: *Jesus dethroned Satan and all his cohorts for me. Satan cannot dominate me. I dominate him. Jesus gave me authority over Satan, and I will use it.*

His Body

Now ye are the body of Christ, and members in particular.
— 1 CORINTHIANS 12:27

We've sometimes prayed about the Lord's work upon the earth like this: "Lord, *You* do this. Lord, *You* do that."

But think about what Jesus said in Matthew 28: "*All power* [authority] *is given unto me in heaven and in earth. Go ye therefore....* " The Lord Jesus Christ conferred the authority on the earth upon us. He commissioned us to go.

Actually, the authority that Christ can exercise on the earth has to be exercised through the Church. The Church is His Body. And the Church is here. Christ is not here. He's at the right hand of the Father. Christ is the Head of the Church, but all of His orders have to be carried out through His Body. Everything Christ does on the earth has to be done through His Body.

You're a member in particular of Christ's Body. He has conferred upon you authority over all the power of the enemy!

Confession: *I am a member in particular of the Body of Christ. I am a worker together with God in the completing of His work upon the earth. I am well equipped. I am endued with power and authority in Jesus' Name. And I will faithfully fulfill my part in God's plan.*

Permitted

Verily I say unto you, Whatsoever ye shall bind on earth shall be bound in heaven: and whatsoever ye shall loose on earth shall be loosed in heaven.

— MATTHEW 18:18

Many things exist because believers *permit* them to — they just don't do anything about them. Sometimes believers don't know they *can* do anything to change these situations.

Years ago, when I was meditating and studying about the authority believers have, I sensed the Lord challenging me. At that time, I had been praying for about fifteen years for my older brother to be saved. I had often prayed and fasted three days at a time for his salvation — but he would get worse instead of better. I'd pray, "God save him. God save him." But nothing ever happened. As I lay across the bed studying on this particular day, I heard the Lord in my spirit. He challenged me: *"You* do something about that situation. You've got the authority. You've got my Name!"

I rose up off that bed and said, "In the Name of Jesus Christ, I break the power of the devil over Dub's life. And I claim his salvation and deliverance!"

In less than two weeks, I got word that Dub had been born again.

Confession: *Jesus said that heaven backs us up in whatever we believers prohibit or permit. In Jesus' Name, I prohibit, or bind, the work of the enemy. And in Jesus' Name I loose, or permit, the power of God to flow in my realm of operation.*

Flee From You

. . . Resist the devil, and he will flee from you.

— JAMES 4:7

Every passage in the New Testament that deals with the devil always instructs you and me to do something about the devil. Never are New Testament believers told to pray that God would do something about the devil!

Here in James 4:7 "you" is the understood subject of the sentence. "*You* resist the devil, and he will flee from *you.*" Notice it's not, "Pray to God for Him to do something about the devil." Nor is it, "Pray that Jesus won't let the devil get you."

Also notice that the Bible doesn't say, "When you feel like it, you can resist the devil, and it will work for you." No. Whether you feel like it or not, the authority still belongs to you. *You can't feel authority; you just exercise it!*

I once sensed in my spirit that there was special significance about the word "flee" in James 4:7. In a huge dictionary I found the definition that seemed to fit what my spirit called for: "To flee: to run from as in terror."

Act on James 4:7. Don't just consider it as a fairy tale, but as the Word of God, which is to be acted upon. If you'll act on it, the devil and all his cohorts will run from you as in terror!

Confession: *I resist the devil according to God's Word. The devil runs from me as in terror. He's scared to death of Jesus Christ — so he's scared to death of me!*

Cast Out Devils

And these signs shall follow them that believe; In my name
shall they cast out devils.... — MARK 16:17

The very first sign Jesus said would follow any
and every believer was: "*... In my name shall they
cast out devils....*"

Jesus wasn't talking necessarily about casting
the devil out of people who are demon possessed.
Jesus was simply saying that believers in His
name would have authority over the devil. They
would break the power of the devil over their own
lives and the lives of their loved ones. They would
be free from the enemy, because they would exercise authority over him.

Notice again that Jesus didn't say a word
about praying to God or Jesus to do something
about devils. Jesus said that believers would do
it. Believers will cast out devils. Believers would
speak with new tongues. Believers would lay their
hands on the sick, and they would recover.

Don't pray that God would lay hands on the
sick — you do it! And don't pray that God would
cast out the devil — you do it!

Confession: *I am a believer, and this sign follows me. In
Jesus' Name I cast out devils. I keep them out of my path.
I break the power of the devil over my life. I break the power
of the devil over the lives of my loved ones. I walk free of
the enemy, because I exercise authority over him.*

Your Domain

For if, because of one man's trespass (lapse, offense) death reigned through that one, much more surely will those who receive [God's] overflowing grace (unmerited favor) and the free gift of righteousness (putting them into right standing with Himself) reign as kings in life through the One, Jesus Christ, the Messiah, the Anointed One.

— ROMANS 5:17 *Amplified*

In the time when Paul wrote this, kings reigned over certain countries or domains.

You are to reign in your domain too. This doesn't mean you're to reign or rule over other people, but you're to rule and reign in your life, in your dominion. You're to rule and reign over circumstances, poverty, sickness, disease — everything that would hinder. You're to reign because you have the authority!

How do you have it? Through the One, Jesus Christ.

Don't let the devil cheat you out of the blessings God intended you should have. God never intended that you should be poverty stricken and destitute. He didn't intend that the devil should rule and reign over your family and dominate them. Just get angry at the devil. Tell him, "Take your hands off my children. You've got no right here. I'm ruling over this domain." If he says anything about it, quote him Romans 5:17.

Confession: *I reign in my domain. I have the authority to do so. I reign by the One, Jesus Christ. The enemy cannot rule over my family. He cannot rule over me!*

To the Church

And hath put all things under his feet, and gave him to be the head over all things to the church, Which is his body . . . .
— EPHESIANS 1:22,23

What a need there is for the Church to awaken to the appreciation of her mighty place and privilege — to be exalted to the place God wants her — to realize she is to rule over the powers of the air!

How often the Church has failed in her ministry of authority, actually bowing down in defeat and being overcome with fear.

"... *and gave him to be the head over all things TO THE CHURCH....*" To the Church! The reason Jesus is Head over all things — the devil, demons, sickness, poverty, and everything else that's evil — is for the benefit of the Church! We need to sit reverently and meditate before these mighty truths so their tremendous meaning can grasp our hearts. In this attitude, the Spirit of Truth can lift us into the place where we can see the full meaning of what God's Word is saying: That God made Christ to be the head over all things for the sake of the Church, so that the Church, through the Head of the Church, might exercise authority over all things.

Confession: *Jesus is my Head. Jesus is Lord over all. Jesus has given me authority over all the hosts of the enemy. Greater is Jesus that is in me than he that is in the world. I am more than a conqueror through Him that loved me and gave Himself for me.*

Firstborn From the Dead

Who [his dear Son] *is the image of the invisible God, the firstborn of every creature: For by him were all things created, that are in heaven, and that are in earth, visible and invisible, whether they be thrones, or dominions, or principalities, or powers: all things were created by him, and for him: And he is before all things, and by him all things consist. And he is the head of the body, the church: who is the beginning, THE FIRSTBORN FROM THE DEAD. . . . For it pleased the Father that in him should all fulness dwell; And, having made peace through the blood of his cross, by him to reconcile all things unto himself. . . .*
— COLOSSIANS 1:15-20

Although He is coequal with the Father, the eternal Son of God accepted a subordinate place and undertook the task of reconciling the world to God through the blood of His cross.

For this purpose Jesus yielded Himself to death (Matt. 27:50). When Jesus was made to be sin (2 Cor. 5:21), He was turned over by God to spiritual death, which is separation from God. This occurred when that heart-breaking cry fell from Jesus' lips, "My God, my God, why hast thou forsaken me?" Jesus' spirit was delivered up for our offenses, that He might be raised for our justification (Rom. 4:25). It was the wisdom of the Father that yielded Jesus, the Righteous One, to death, that our debt might be paid, and Jesus might become THE FIRSTBORN FROM THE DEAD!

Confession: *Thank You, Jesus, for dying for my sins. Thank you, Jesus, that you paid my debt so that I might be set free!*

Stripped

And having spoiled principalities and powers, he made a shew of them openly, triumphing over them in it.

— COLOSSIANS 2:15

And the hostile princes and rulers He shook off from Himself, and boldly displayed them as His conquests....

— COLOSSIANS 2:15 *Weymouth*

The Bible teaches us here that Jesus put Satan to nought and He triumphed over him. Another translation reads, "He stripped him." What did He strip Satan of? His authority over man.

When Jesus put Satan to nought and stripped him of his authority, it was you in Christ who did that work. Christ acted in your stead — in your place. He did it for you.

What Christ did was marked to your credit. He did it as your substitute. (He did it in your place, and God marked it to your credit as though you were the one who did it!)

No, we're not bragging about what you are in the flesh. (You don't amount to much in the flesh.) We're talking about who you are *in Christ.*

You can say, "*In Christ*, I conquered Satan. I stripped him of his authority. And *when Jesus arose from the dead, I arose with Him!*"

Confession: *Christ Jesus satisfied the claims of Justice against me. He paid the penalty of sin for me. He stripped the hosts of darkness of their authority over me. Satan, therefore, has no dominion over me!*

Paralyzed

Forasmuch then as the children are partakers of flesh and blood, he also himself likewise took part of the same; that through death he might destroy him that had the power of death, that is, the devil.

— HEBREWS 2:14

. . . that He might paralyse him that held the dominion of death, That is the Adversary.

— HEBREWS 2:14 *Rotherham*

Jesus put to naught the hosts of darkness! He paralyzed their death-dealing power! And when Jesus met John the Revelator on the Isle of Patmos, Jesus said, *"I am he that liveth, and was dead; and, behold, I am alive for evermore, Amen; and have the keys of hell and of death"* (Rev.1:18).

Keys represent authority. Jesus conquered Satan and stripped him of his authority. Jesus was the master of all hell!

But Jesus did not conquer Satan for Himself. He conquered him for us. It was as though you and I personally had met Satan and had conquered him, stripped him of his authority, and stood a master over him.

Confession: *Jesus is my Head. Jesus is Lord over all. Jesus conquered Satan for me. Jesus stripped Satan of his authority over me. In the eyes of heaven, hell, and this universe, it was as though I personally had met Satan and had conquered him, stripped him of his authority, and stood a master over him. Therefore, in Christ Jesus, I am more than a conqueror. I am a holder of authority. I stand a master over Satan and all his cohorts!*

The Agent: God

And ye are complete in him, which is the head of all principality and power. . . . Buried with him in baptism, wherein also ye are risen with him through the faith of the operation of God, who hath raised him from the dead. And you . . . hath he quickened together with him. . . .

— COLOSSIANS 2:10,12,13

Notice the expression "through the faith of the operation of God." Jesus was quickened (made alive) by the faith of the operation of God — and we were made alive at the same time. It was God who raised Jesus from the dead. It was God who gave Jesus a Name above every name. It was God who blotted out "the handwriting of ordinances" against us, took it out of the way, and nailed it to His cross (Col. 2:14). It was God who stripped the powers of darkness of their authority and handed it to the Son (Col. 2:15). And it was God who quickened us "together with Him."

In the mind of God, legally speaking, it was when Jesus was quickened and made alive, that we were recreated. *"For we are his workmanship, created in Christ Jesus. . . "* (Eph. 2:10). This fact of our re-creation becomes a vital reality in our lives when we are individually born again (made new creatures).

Raised with Christ! Quickened with Him! Seated with Him! (Eph. 2:4-6).

Confession: *Through the faith of the operation of God, I was quickened together with Christ and was seated with Him in heavenly places.*

Analogy

*And he is the head of the body, the church: who is the begin-
ning, the firstborn from the dead; that in all things he might
have the preeminence.* — COLOSSIANS 1:18

Here's where we believers have missed it!
We've recognized that Jesus is the Head of the
Church, and we've exalted Him to His position of
Power, all right. But we've failed to see that the
Head is wholly dependent upon its body for carrying out its plans. We've failed to see that we are
seated with Christ in heavenly places. We've failed
to see that Jesus has authority over Satan's
power. If this authority is ever exercised, it will
have to be exercised through the Body. We've been
so sure that *we* couldn't do anything, that we've
left everything up to Christ the Head of the
Church — and the Head is powerless without the
Body.

Take your own physical head as an example.
It is powerless to carry out any of its plans without
the cooperation of the body. Your head might see
a songbook on a rack in front of you, but unless
your body cooperates, your head will never be able
to sing from that book.

The ministry God wants to accomplish through
His Son in this world will be carried out through
the Body of Christ. And we — the Body of Christ
— have the same authority the Head has!

Confession: *The ministry God wants to accomplish through
His Son in this world will be carried out through the Body
of Christ. I am a member of the Body, and I will exercise
my authority!*

What Ye Will

If ye abide in me, and my words abide in you, ye shall ask what ye will, and it shall be done unto you.

— JOHN 15:7

The Lord has said to me as I prayed about the impending death of loved ones, "Whatever you say about it, that's what I'll do."

In one particular case, as I pled my rights in prayer concerning a situation, the Lord came to me in a vision and said, "All right, I'm going to give them _____ more years. And I'm going to do it just because you asked Me to. No earthly father ever desired to do more for his children than I do for mine, if they would only let Me."

Why doesn't God just do it?

Because we must cooperate with God in faith!

The idea that God is a tyrant who rules over people, knocks heads together, and does what He wants to, whether man cooperates or not, is pure ignorance.

We have a part to play! And, thank God, we can take our rightful place. The Lord Jesus Christ — Head over all things to His Body — is hindered in His mighty plans and workings because His Body fails to appreciate the deep meaning of His exaltation, and the fact that we are seated with Him at the right hand of the Father!

Confession: *I abide in Christ, and His words abide in me. Therefore, I ask what I will, and it shall be done unto me!*

Taking Your Place

If ye then be risen with Christ, seek those things which are above, where Christ sitteth on the right hand of God. Set your affection on things above, not on things on the earth.
— COLOSSIANS 3:1,2

The elevation of the believer to be seated with Christ at the right hand of the Father took place potentially at the resurrection (Eph. 2:5,6). Meditate on this passage until it becomes real to you. Remember, every heavenly blessing is yours (Eph. 1:3). But you have to take your place there to enjoy them. The believer whose eyes have been opened to his throne rights in Christ may: (1) Accept his seat, and (2) Begin to exercise the spiritual authority that seating confers on him.

The devil bitterly resents our entrance into his domain. He has been used to exercising authority and ruling over someone's life, so he will concentrate his forces against us when we come into these mighty truths. And no truth encounters such opposition as the truth of the authority of the believer!

The only place of safety is to be seated with Christ in heavenly places, far above all principality, power, might, and dominion. If the believer abides steadfastly, by faith, in this place, he cannot be touched by the enemy. So take your seat in heavenly places and keep it!

Confession: *I set my affection on heavenly facts. I keep myself mindful that I am seated with Christ in heavenly places far above the enemy!*

The Armor

Wherefore take unto you the whole armour of God, that ye may be able to withstand in the evil day, and having done all, to stand. — EPHESIANS 6:13

The message of the armor (Eph. 6:10-18) tells us how to take our place and maintain it against the devil.

"Stand therefore, having your loins girt about with truth...." The girdle of truth is a clear understanding of God's Word. It holds the rest of the armor in place like a soldier's belt.

"... and having on the breastplate of righteousness." The breastplate has two meanings: (1) Jesus is our righteousness, so we put Him on; (2) The breastplate represents our active obedience to the Word of God.

"And your feet shod with the preparation of the gospel of peace." This is faithful ministry in proclaiming the Word of God.

"Above all, taking the shield of faith, wherewith ye shall be able to quench all the fiery darts of the wicked." This is complete safety by faith in the blood. No power of the enemy can penetrate the blood!

"And take the helmet of salvation...." This is the covering of our Lord Jesus Christ.

"... the sword of the Spirit, which is the word of God." All other parts of the armor are for protection (defense); this one is to be used offensively against the enemy.

"Praying always with all prayer and supplication in the Spirit...." You've got on the armor. Now you're ready for the prayer fight.

Confession: *Confess yourself in the armor. Say, "I stand, therefore, having my loins girt about with truth...," etc.*

Unseen Forces

For we wrestle not against flesh and blood, but against principalities, against powers, against the rulers of the darkness of this world, against spiritual wickedness in high places.
— EPHESIANS 6:12

We are called upon to bind unseen forces. We have authority over the devil and evil spirits. But we do not have authority over our fellow men or their wills.

Years ago, a pastor friend of mine accompanied me from Fort Worth to a campmeeting in California. This man had diabetes, and he had to check his urine every morning for sugar content to see how much insulin he would need for his daily injection.

As we were leaving for California, I said, "You won't register any sugar as long as you're with me." He looked at me as if he didn't believe me, but in the almost two weeks he was with me, he never registered any sugar, even though he ate pies and cakes. He later told me he was home for three days before he registered sugar again.

Why? I took authority over his sickness. I had control over unseen forces, but I didn't have control over his will. As long as he was with me, and this unseen force was in my presence, I could control it. I tried to convince him he could do the same thing, but he expected it to come back and it did.

Confession: *I have authority over all unseen forces in my realm of domain. And I bind them and stop their activity in Jesus' Name!*

Blinded

But if our gospel be hid, it is hid to them that are lost: In whom the god of this world hath blinded the minds of them which believe not, lest the light of the glorious gospel of Christ, who is the image of God, should shine unto them.
— 2 CORINTHIANS 4:3,4

No man in his right mind would speed down the highway at 100 miles per hour past flashing red lights and signs that said, "Danger! Danger! Bridge Out!" But a man who was drunk or on drugs would.

Likewise, no man in his right mind would go through life and plunge off into eternity and hell, lost. But people do it. Why? Because the devil has them doped and blinded.

In the case of my Brother Dub's salvation, I realized it was the devil who had bound Dub and was keeping him from being saved. So I said, "Satan, in the Name of Jesus Christ, I break your power over my brother Dub's life, and I claim his deliverance and salvation!"

We do not have control over human wills, but we do have control over evil spirits that bind and blind men. I'm convinced this is an area we're going to know more about and take advantage of in the future.

Confession: *The god of this world will not blind the eyes of my loved ones, because I will take the Name of Jesus and break his power over them!*

Foundation

Study to shew thyself approved unto God, a workman that needeth not to be ashamed, rightly dividing the word of truth.
— 2 TIMOTHY 2:15

Someone who reads about how I took my authority over the spirits binding my brother might say, "I believe I'll *try* that." It won't work if you *try* it. I didn't just *try* it — I *did* it!

Just because someone sees a traffic policeman exercising his authority doesn't mean they can run out in front of the cars and say, "I believe I'll try that." No one would obey them. Now, if they would put on a policeman's uniform and put a whistle in their mouth, people would stop. They would recognize the authority behind the policeman.

Believers sometimes hear how someone else used their authority, and they think, *I'll try that because I heard him say it. It worked for him, so it will work for me.* Satan knows they are not convinced of their authority, and when they try to act on God's Word without really having that Word built into their spirits, and without having the solid foundation of it built into their lives, the devil will defeat them — and defeat them soundly.

But when you've built a foundation of the Word of God in you, and you act on God's Word, you'll defeat the devil in every combat!

Confession: *I study to show myself approved unto God. I build the truths of God's Word into my life and spirit. I am convinced by God's Word of my authority. I cannot be defeated. And the devil knows it!*

Lord, Teach Us To Pray

And it came to pass, that, as he was praying in a certain place, when he ceased, one of his disciples said unto him, Lord, teach us to pray.... — LUKE 11:1

Someone said, "It is more important that men learn to pray than that they gain a college education." Notice he did not say that having an education is not important; he said that learning to pray is more important.

I feel so sorry for people who don't know how to pray. When the crises of life come, they know how to say words — but just spouting off words into the atmosphere isn't praying! Simply talking into the air is not praying. Taking up twenty minutes on a Sunday morning giving God a homily on what His duties are toward the church is not praying. And giving the congregation a lecture pretending to be praying to God is not praying.

Christianity, from a practical side, is a living religion whose believers are in touch with the living God who hears and answers prayer. And prayer may be defined as joining forces with God the Father — fellowshipping with Him — carrying out His will upon the earth.

It is of utmost importance that all Christians — *including you* — learn how to pray!

Confession: *I am in touch with the living God who hears and answers prayer. I fellowship with Him. I join forces with Him in carrying out His will upon the earth.*

Limiting God

Yea, they turned back and tempted God, and limited the Holy One of Israel. — PSALM 78:41

Can you limit God? The Bible says Israel did. And we have limited Him. We have limited God with our prayer life!

John Wesley, founder of Methodism, said, "It seems that God is limited by our prayer life. He can do nothing for humanity unless someone asks Him to do it."

Why is this?

God made the world and the fullness thereof. Then God made man and gave man dominion over all the works of His hands. Adam was made the god of this world. Adam, however, committed high treason and sold out to Satan. Then Satan became the god of this world (2 Cor. 4:4).

God didn't just move in and destroy Satan. If He had, Satan could have accused God of doing the same thing he had done. But God devised a plan of salvation. And He sent His Son, whom Satan could not and did not touch, to consummate that plan. Through Jesus, God redeemed mankind!

Now authority has been restored to us through Jesus Christ — and when we ask God, then He can and will move. That is why it seems He can do nothing unless someone asks Him to do it.

Confession: *I take my place in prayer. I join forces with my Father in carrying out His will upon the earth!*

Covenant Friend

And Abraham drew near, and said, Wilt thou also destroy the righteous with the wicked? Peradventure there be fifty righteous within the city: wilt thou also destroy and not spare the place for the fifty righteous that are therein? That be far from thee to do after this manner, to slay the righteous with the wicked: and that the righteous should be as the wicked, that be far from thee: Shall not the Judge of all the earth do right? — GENESIS 18:23-25

God refused to destroy Sodom and Gomorrah until He had talked it over with Abraham, His blood covenant friend!

Abraham's prayer in this eighteenth chapter of Genesis is one of the most suggestive and illuminating prayers in the Old Testament. Abraham was taking his place in the covenant that God had made with him — the Old Covenant, the Old Testament.

Abraham, through the covenant, had received rights and privileges we understand little about. The covenant Abraham had just solemnized with the Lord Jehovah gave Abraham a legal standing with God. Therefore, we hear Abraham speak plainly as he intercedes for Sodom and Gomorrah, "Shall not the Judge of all the earth do right?"

Confession: *I have a covenant with God, the New Covenant. I have covenant rights and privileges. I have a standing with God. I commune with God. I use my covenant rights and privileges in prayer. I join forces with my Father in carrying out His will and plan upon the earth.*

A Better Covenant

But now hath he [Jesus] obtained a more excellent ministry, by how much also he is the mediator of a better covenant, which was established upon better promises.

— HEBREWS 8:6

All through the Old Testament, we find men who understood and took their place in the covenant. Joshua could open the River Jordan. He could command time to stand still. Elijah could bring fire out of heaven to consume not only the sacrifice, but the altar as well. David's mighty men were utterly shielded from death in time of war as long as they remembered the covenant. When you read about them, you think you're reading about "supermen."

Nearly all the prayers in the Old Testament were prayed by covenant men. Those prayers *had* to be answered!

The believer today has the same covenant rights as believers who lived under the Old Covenant. In fact, we have a *better* covenant established upon better promises. Therefore, we ought to be able to do all that they did and *more,* because we have a New Covenant, a better covenant, established on greater promises.

Confession: *Through Jesus, I have a covenant with God. It is a better covenant, based on better promises. I have better covenant rights than Abraham, Joshua, Elijah, and David had. I take my place as a New Testament believer in prayer. My prayers have to be answered!*

Plead Your Case

Put me in remembrance: let us plead together: declare thou,
that thou mayest be justified. — ISAIAH 43:26

"*Put me in remembrance. . . .*" What does God
mean by that? It means that we are to remind God
of His promises about prayer.

When you pray, stand before the throne of God
and remind Him of His promises. Lay your case
legally before Him, and plead it as a lawyer. A
lawyer is continually bringing up law and prece-
dent. You bring up God's Word. Bring up His
covenant promises.

The margin of my *King James* reference Bible
shows "set forth thy cause" as another meaning
of "declare thou" in this verse. God is asking you
to bring His Word; to put Him in remembrance,
and to plead your covenant rights. This is a
challenge from God to lay your case before Him!

If your children are unsaved — or whatever it
is you are praying about — find Scriptures which
cover your case. Then lay the matter before God.
Be definite in your requests. Find Scriptures that
definitely promise you those things you need.
When you come to God according to His Word,
His Word does not fail.

Confession: *I accept the challenge of the covenant-keeping*
God! I put God in remembrance of His promises. I plead
my case. I set forth my cause legally. I find Scriptures that
cover my case, and I lay the matter before God. I come
according to God's Word, and God's Word does not fail!

He Keeps His Word

For as the rain cometh down, and the snow from heaven, and returneth not thither, but watereth the earth, and maketh it bring forth and bud, that it may give seed to the sower, and bread to the eater: So shall my word be that goeth forth out of my mouth: it shall not return unto me void, but it shall accomplish that which I please, and it shall prosper in the thing whereto I sent it.

— ISAIAH 55:10,11

Isaiah 55:11 is a verse you should continually use in prayer. It is the very backbone of the prayer life. No word that has gone forth from God can return to Him void.

God said, "*. . . I will hasten my word to perform it*" (Jer. 1:12). A marginal note in the King James version reads, "I will watch over my word to peform it."

God will make His Word good if you dare to stand by it!

The greatest answers to prayer I have received came when I brought God's Word to Him and reminded Him of what He had said.

Praise God, He keeps His Word!

Confession: *God's Word shall not return to Him void, but it shall accomplish that which God pleases, and it shall prosper in the thing whereto God sent it. I bring God's Word to Him in prayer. And God makes it good. He keeps His Word. And I receive the benefits.*

Prayer Fruit

If ye abide in me, and my words abide in you, ye shall ask what ye will, and it shall be done unto you. Herein is my Father glorified, that ye bear much fruit; so shall ye be my disciples. — JOHN 15:7,8

"If ye abide in me. . . ." If we are born again, we do abide in Christ. If Jesus had said that and that alone, we would have had it made, but Jesus said, *". . . AND my words abide in you. . . ."*

Jesus' words abide in us in the measure that they govern our lives — in the measure that we act upon them.

If Jesus' words abide in us, we are bound to have faith, because the Bible says, *"So then faith cometh by hearing, and hearing by the word of God"* (Rom. 10:17). It would be impossible for Jesus' words to abide in someone and that person not have faith!

Unbelief, or doubt, is a result of ignorance of the Word of God. If we live the Word, then when we come to pray, that Word dwells in us so richly that it becomes Jesus' Word on our lips. It will be as the Father's words were on the lips of Jesus.

Confession: *I abide in Christ. And His words abide in me. I hide His words in my heart. I believe them. I pray them. When I come to prayer, the Word that dwells in my heart becomes God's Word on my lips, and it cannot return to God void. It will accomplish what it promises!*

According to His Will

And this is the confidence that we have in him, that, if we ask any thing according to his will, he heareth us: And if we know that he hear us, whatsoever we ask, we know that we have the petitions that we desired of him.

— 1 JOHN 5:14,15

People have remembered John's phrase "according to his will," and they thought they had to pray, "Lord, do this or that, *if it be thy will.*" But inserting this expression into a prayer when God's Word already states that what we're praying for is his will — is confessing that we don't believe God's Word. And that kind of praying will not work.

How can we find out what God's will is?

God's Word is His will! We can find out God's will for us in the Bible — because the Bible is God's will, His covenant, and His testament. And it is God's will for us to have whatever God has provided for us!

First we must find the Scriptures that reveal God's will for us. Then we can go before God with great boldness: "*. . . this is the CONFIDENCE that we have in Him. . . .*" When we pray for things that God's Word tells us *are* His will, we *know* that he hears us! And when we *know* God hears us, we *know* we have the petitions we ask of Him. We *know* we have them, praise God!

Confession: *I have this boldness toward God: When I ask anything according to God's Word, I know He hears me! And I know that when God hears me, I have the petitions I desired of Him!*

62

Saving the Lost

The Lord is ... longsuffering to us-ward, not willing that any should perish, but that all should come to repentance.
— 2 PETER 3:9

We know that saving the lost is God's will — because it was to save the lost that Jesus laid down His life.

Therefore, knowing this, we would not pray, "God, save my mother, *if it is your will.* Don't let her go to hell, *if it is your will. If it is not your will,* let her go on to hell."

No! Why? *Because we know God's will in the matter.* God's will — His Word — makes it clear in such Scriptures as John 3:16 and Second Peter 3:9 that God's will is for men and women to be saved. Therefore, we can pray for the lost with great boldness.

Believers especially can exercise great authority in praying for the salvation of their families. I used some of the Scriptures we have been studying as I prayed for my relatives. I said something like this: "This is the confidence that we have in God, that, if we ask anything according to His will, He hears us. What I am asking for is according to God's will; therefore, He hears me. That is what the Word says. *'And if we know that he hear us, whatsoever we ask, we know that we have the petitions that we desired of him.'* According to the Word, then, I have that petition."

Then I stopped asking and started thanking God. It's amazing how it works. I don't mean that your entire family will necessarily come to the Lord overnight, but as you stand in faith, thanking God, they will come.

Confession: *I can pray in faith for the lost, because I know God's will in the matter!*

Supplying Our Needs

But my God shall supply all your need according to his riches in glory by Christ Jesus.

— PHILIPPIANS 4:19

It is God's will that our needs be met. *All* of them!

Philippians 4:19 includes all of your needs (*all* means *all!*), whether spiritual, physical, material, or financial.

Believe that!

Lest someone think that God is not concerned about our financial needs, this verse is set in a context which discusses material and financial affairs. Read it and you will see that the Philippians had taken up an offering of money and goods to send to other Christians. Paul was telling them, "Because you have given to others and have helped them, my God shall supply all your need." So Paul was talking about material and financial matters.

With what boldness, then, we can pray for finances to meet our obligations! Having all of our needs met is according to God's will!

Confession: *When I pray concerning finances, I pray according to God's Word — His will. Therefore, I am confident that God hears me. That's what His Word says. And if I know that God hears whatever I ask of Him, I know that I have the petition I desired of Him. According to the Word of God, I have my petition. And I thank God for it!*

The Good

If ye be willing and obedient, ye shall eat the good of the land.
— ISAIAH 1:19

If you are willing and obedient, it is God's will that you have the best. (Of course, you can't walk in disobedience and enjoy the good things of God.)

God is not a miser or a tightwad. And He didn't put everything here in this world for the devil and his crowd to enjoy.

Some people have the idea that if you're a Christian, you should never have anything, financially or materially speaking. They believe that you should go through life poor and beaten down.

But Jesus said, *"If ye then, being evil* [natural], *know how to give good gifts unto your children, HOW MUCH MORE shall your Father which is in heaven give good things to them that ask him?"* (Matt. 7:11).

Oh, God wants to give us good gifts! He wants us to have the best! He wants us to prosper and have the good things of this life! But we must cooperate with Him.

Confession: *I am willing to love and serve God my Father. I am obedient to walk in the light of His Word, His will. Therefore, I shall eat the good of the land. And with confidence I can pray for the good things in life, because it is my Father's will that I have them.*

His Riches

A good man leaveth an inheritance to his children's children: and the wealth of the sinner is laid up for the just.
— PROVERBS 13:22

The Lord Jesus said to me once as he came and sat by my bedside and talked to me for an hour and a half about being led of the Spirit, "My Spirit will lead all of my children. The Bible says, *'For as many as are led by the Spirit of God, they are the sons of God'* (Rom. 8:14). I will lead you, and not only you, but any child of God. I will show you what to do with your money. I will show you how to invest it. In fact, if you will listen to me, I will make you rich. I am not opposed to my children being rich. I am opposed to their being covetous."

(Someone could be covetous and not have a dime.)

People misquote the Bible when they claim that it says, "Money is the root of all evil." But the Bible doesn't say that at all. It says, *"For the love of money is the root of all evil. . ."* (1 Tim. 6:10).

It is all right to have money. It is wrong for money to have you!

Confession: *I am a child of God. I am led by the Spirit of God. My trust is in God, not in riches. But I trust God to lead me concerning my finances. I honor God with tithes and offerings of all that I have. And all of my needs are supplied according to God's riches in glory by Christ Jesus.*

Healing: God's Will

For I came down from heaven, not to do mine own will,
but the will of him that sent me. — JOHN 6:38

Healing the sick is God's will.

Yet Christians who need healing have said to me, "Maybe God put this sickness on me for some purpose."

Did Jesus ever put sickness on anybody? When people came to Jesus for healing, did He ever turn even one away, saying, "No, it's not my will. Just suffer a little longer. Wait until your piety gets deepened enough"?

No! Not once!

Do you want to know what God is like? Look at Jesus. Do you want to see God at work? Look at Jesus! Did Jesus go about making people sick? No! He went about doing good and healing (Acts 10:38). Do you want to know the will of God? Look at Jesus. Jesus is the will of God in action.

We can pray for healing with great confidence — knowing it is the will of God!

Confession: *When I pray concerning healing, I know that I pray according to God's will. It is God's will that we have what Jesus bought for us. Therefore, I am confident that God hears me. And since I know that God hears me, I know that I have the petition I desire of Him. And I thank Him for it!*

Don't Blame God

*... he that hath seen me hath seen the Father.... Believest
thou not that I am in the Father, and the Father in me?
the words that I speak unto you I speak not of myself: but
the Father that dwelleth in me, he doeth the works.*

— JOHN 14:9,10

Many of the laws that govern this earth today
came into being when Adam sinned and the curse
came upon the earth.

Because people don't understand this, they
accuse God of causing accidents, sickness, the
death of loved ones, storms, catastrophes, earth-
quakes, floods, etc. Even insurance policies — and
it makes me angry every time I see it — call such
things "acts of God." They are not acts of God!
They are acts of the devil!

Jesus set aside these natural laws to bless
humanity. We don't see Jesus bringing any storms
on people. In fact, we see Jesus stilling the storms.
Therefore, God didn't send the storm. Jesus
wouldn't rebuke something God did! But Jesus
did rebuke what the devil stirred up.

*When you see Jesus at work, you see God at
work.* Jesus' description of the Father, and His
statement that "... *he that hath seen me hath seen
the Father...,*" (John 14:9) make it impossible to
accept the teaching that sickness and disease are
from God. The very nature of God refutes such an
idea!

Confession: *God is love. And I don't blame love for what
the devil does. I look at Jesus, and I see love at work.*

Purpose

. . . For this purpose the Son of God was manifested, that he might destroy the works of the devil.

—1 JOHN 3:8

During the Korean Conflict, I read an article by a well-known newspaper columnist. He said, in effect, "I don't claim to be a Christian, but I'm not an atheist or an agnostic, either. The atheist says there is no God. The agnostic says there may be a God; he doesn't know. I believe there is a God. I don't believe everything just happened into being. What hinders me from being a Christian is what I hear preachers say. They say that God is running everything. Well, if He is, He's sure got things in a mess!"

Then the columnist alluded to the wars, children being killed, poverty, disease, etc., that plague our world. He said, "I believe there is a Supreme Being somewhere, and that everything He made was beautiful and good. I can't believe these other things are the works of God."

No, those things came with the fall, when Satan became the god of this world (2 Cor. 4:4). And the Bible teaches that when Satan is finally eliminated from the earth, there will be nothing here that will hurt or destroy. It ought to be obvious where all that hurts or destroys comes from. If evil came from God, we would still have it after Satan is destroyed from the scene, because God will still be here. But we know that evil does not come from God.

Confession: *The Son of God was manifested so that He might destroy the works of the devil. As part of Christ's Body, I take my authority over the works of the devil!*

Source of Sickness

And ought not this woman, being a daughter of Abraham, whom Satan hath bound, lo, these eighteen years, be loosed from this bond on the sabbath day?

— LUKE 13:16

The Bible is progressive revelation. It is in the New Testament that we get full light, full truth, and full revelation. There Jesus plainly taught that sickness is of the devil, not of God.

In Luke 13, we see Jesus going into the synagogue on the Sabbath. A woman was there whose body was bowed together in a fixed position. She couldn't straighten up. She may have had arthritis. Jesus called her to come to Him, and said, "Woman, thou art loosed from thine infirmity!" Then Jesus laid hands on her, and immediately she stood straight. The ruler of the synagogue, like the leaders of some churches today, got angry about it!

Then, as recorded in our text, Jesus elaborated on the fact that Satan is the author of sickness. Jesus made three enlightening statements: (1) The woman ought to be loosed; she ought not to be bound; she ought to be free from this physical infirmity. (2) It was Satan who had bound her, not God. (3) The reason this woman ought to be loosed was because she was a daughter of Abraham.

Confession: *Since Satan is the author of sickness, I ought to walk free from sickness. And Jesus has made the provision for me to do so. Divine health is my covenant right!*

Healing Is Good

How God anointed Jesus of Nazareth with the Holy Ghost and with power: who went about doing good, and healing all that were oppressed of the devil; for God was with him.

— ACTS 10:38

Who anointed Jesus of Nazareth? God did! And Jesus said, "*. . . the Father that dwelleth in me, he doeth the works*" (John 14:10). How did God do these works of healings through Jesus? By anointing Jesus with the Holy Spirit and with healing power.

What did Jesus do with the anointing that God had anointed Him with? *He went about doing good!* And what was the good Jesus did? *Healing!*

Therefore, it was actually God healing the people when Jesus healed, because it was God who had anointed Jesus. God is in the healing business! He's not in the sickness business!

Who was it Jesus healed? All that were oppressed of the devil. All! *ALL!* Everybody healed under the ministry of Jesus was oppressed of the devil. (This doesn't mean that everybody had an evil spirit, but it does mean that the devil is behind all sickness.)

Yet to hear some people talk — even ministers — they would lead you to believe that God and the devil had swapped jobs in the last 2,000 years, and God is putting sickness on people, and the devil is healing them. But, no! The devil is the same devil he has always been. And God is the same God!

Confession: *Satan is the oppressor, not God. Jesus is the Deliverer!*

Set Against Sickness

And he said unto them, Go ye into all the world, and preach the gospel to every creature. . . . And these signs shall follow them that believe; In my name . . . they shall lay hands on the sick, and they shall recover.

— MARK 16:15,17,18

Let's stop and analyze something here: Just which of the sick did Jesus say we were to lay hands on?

Jesus just said "the sick" — period.

Then, if God were the author of sickness — if God did put sickness and disease on people — if it were the will of God for some to be sick — this statement would be confusing. Because in it, Jesus authorized us to lay hands on ALL the sick.

If God weren't in the healing business, Jesus would have had to say something like, "Lay your hands on those that it is the will of God to heal, and they shall recover. And those it isn't — they won't recover."

But, no! God set the Church against sickness — period!

Confession: *God is in the healing business. God is not in the sickness business. God is in the delivering business. God is not in the bondage business. I refuse to allow the enemy to try to get me to accept sickness or bondage as being from God. Satan is the author of sickness. God has set me against sickness!*

Any

Is any sick among you? let him call for the elders of the church; and let them pray over him, anointing him with oil in the name of the Lord: And the prayer of faith shall save the sick, and the Lord shall raise him up; and if he have committed sins, they shall be forgiven him.

— JAMES 5:14,15

"*Is any sick among you?*"

Among whom?

The Church!

Then it *must* be God's will to heal "any" of the sick in the Church!

And it *can't* be God's will for "any" in the Church to stay sick!

"But, Brother Hagin, you've forgotten," one person said.

"Forgotten what?"

"The Bible says that if we *suffer* with Him, we'll reign with Him."

"No, I haven't forgotten," I explained. "Let's read it again: '. . . *if . . . we suffer WITH HIM . . .* ' (Rom. 8:17). Suffer what: Pneumonia? Cancer? Tuberculosis? No! Jesus didn't suffer from any of these things."

What did Jesus suffer? *Persecution.* And you will, too, if you live right. Especially if you preach divine healing, the gifts of the Spirit, and faith. I've suffered persecution for more than half a century, but I haven't suffered sickness and disease.

Confession: *It is God's will for the Church, His Body, to walk in divine health. It is God's will for me to be well!*

Chastening

That he might sanctify and cleanse it [the Church] *with the washing of water by the word.*

— EPHESIANS 5:26

"You've forgotten," somebody said to me.

"What did I forget?"

"Right over there in the Book of Hebrews it says, '*. . . whom the Lord loveth he chasteneth . . .*'" (Heb. 12:6).

"No, I didn't forget. That verse is still in there. But it doesn't say, 'whom the Lord loveth He makes sick.'"

People put their own interpretation on verses. "Chasten" in the Greek means "to child train, to educate." You train your children. You send them to school. But did you ever tell the teacher, "If Johnny doesn't do right, knock his eye out"? Or, "If Johnny is disobedient, break his leg"? Or, "Give him cancer"? No! That isn't the way you discipline or train a child! And that's not the way God does it!

Confession: *I am trained by the Word and the Spirit of God. I am educated by the Word and the Spirit of God. I am disciplined by the Word and the Spirit of God. With the washing of water by the Word, I am cleansed!*

Every Good Gift

Every good gift and every perfect gift is from above, and cometh down from the Father of lights, with whom is no variableness, neither shadow of turning.

— JAMES 1:17

What is good?

Acts 10:38 says that Jesus went about doing good *and healing*. Healing is good! Sickness is not good. Every healing comes down from the Father. Every sickness does not come down from the Father.

In the first place, where in the world would God get sickness to put on you? He doesn't have any in heaven. He would have to go borrow some from the devil! (You can't give somebody something you don't have.) The Bible says there is no sickness in heaven. Therefore, sickness can't come from heaven.

What does come down from heaven?

Every good gift and every perfect gift!

Confession: *Every good gift and every perfect gift is from above, and comes down from my Father, the Father of lights. Only good gifts can come down from God, for God is good, and heaven holds only good. There is no sickness in heaven. Therefore, sickness cannot come from God. Healing comes from God. So I purpose to receive only what my Father gives — healing!*

How About Job?

And the Lord turned the captivity of Job, when he prayed for his friends: also the Lord gave Job twice as much as he had before. — JOB 42:10

"But you've forgotten, Brother Hagin, that God made Job sick," someone said.

"No, He didn't — the devil did."

"Yeah, but God gave him permission!"

But God didn't commission Job's problems. God will *permit* you to rob a gas station (*you* have free will), but He won't *commission* you to do it.

Actually, God has only given the devil "permission" in a sense. If you allow Satan to attack you, God will permit it, because Satan is the god of this world (2 Cor. 4:4), and you are living on his territory. Job himself opened the door to the devil by being afraid. Job said, *"For the thing which I greatly feared is come upon me, and that which I was afraid of is come unto me"* (Job 3:25).

Many Bible scholars agree that the entire Book of Job took place over a nine- to eighteen-month period. Afterwards, we see that God turned Job's *captivity.* Therefore, when Job was sick, he was in captivity to the devil. When Job was in poverty, he was in captivity to the devil. But God turned Job's captivity! God gave Job twice as much as he had to begin with. That's God at work!

Confession: *God turns our captivity! He doesn't put us in bondage. God sets us free! Through Jesus, I am free! I will never accept sickness and disease as being from God! I know where it comes from — and I stand against it!*

What About Paul's Thorn?

But if ye will not drive out the inhabitants of the land from before you; then it shall come to pass, that those which ye let remain of them shall be pricks in your eyes, and thorns in your sides, and shall vex you in the land wherein ye dwell.
— NUMBERS 33:55

"Don't you remember, though, Brother Hagin — Paul was sick all his life."

"No, I don't remember that."

"But he had *a thorn in the flesh.*"

"Where did you ever read in the Bible that a thorn in the flesh is sickness? Nowhere!"

Go to the Scriptures. See how the Bible uses that term. In the Old Testament, God said to Israel, in effect, "If you don't kill those Canaanites when you possess the land, they will be thorns in your side. They will torment you" (Num. 33:55; Joshua 23:13; Judges 2:3).

Paul tells exactly what the thorn was: "... *the messenger of Satan to buffet me...*" (2 Cor. 12:7). Everywhere Paul went to preach, this evil spirit went before and behind him, and stirred up everything it could. (And Paul couldn't command the evil spirit to leave the earth, because the devil has the right to be here until Adam's lease runs out.)

So there is no separating sickness and disease from Satan — he causes them. Jesus' attitude toward sickness was uncompromising warfare against Satan.

Confession: *Since sickness and disease are of the devil, I follow in the footsteps and attitude of Jesus, and deal with them as Jesus did!*

The Lord That Healeth

... If thou wilt diligently hearken to the voice of the Lord thy God, and wilt do that which is right in his sight, and wilt give ear to his commandments, and keep all his statutes, I will put [literal Hebrew: I will permit] *none of these diseases upon thee, which I have brought* [permitted] *upon the Egyptians: for I am the Lord that healeth thee.*

— EXODUS 15:26

When Israel crossed the Red Sea and started toward their homeland, the Lord spoke these words to them and revealed Himself as Jehovah-Rapha. Jehovah-Rapha translated is, "I am the Lord thy Physician," or *"I am the Lord that healeth thee."* God didn't put diseases upon Israel or upon the Egyptians. It is Satan, the god of this world, who makes man sick. Jehovah declares that He is the Healer.

F. F. Bosworth, in his book *Christ the Healer,* said, "This name [Jehovah-Rapha] is given to reveal to us our *redemptive* privilege of being healed. ... The fact is, that the very first covenant God gave after the passage of the Red Sea, which was so distinctively typical of our redemption, was the covenant of healing, and it was at this time that God revealed Himself as our Physician, by the first *redemptive* and covenant name, Jehovah-Rapha, 'I am the Lord that healeth thee.' This is not only a promise, it is 'a statute and an ordinance.' "

Confession: *Jehovah-Rapha* — *"I am the Lord that healeth thee"* — *is the name of my Lord.*

Covenant Blessing

And ye shall serve the Lord your God, and he shall bless thy bread, and thy water; and I will take sickness away from the midst of thee. There shall nothing cast their young, nor be barren, in thy land: the number of thy days I will fulfil.

— EXODUS 23:25,26

As long as Israel walked in the covenant, there was no sickness among them. There is no record of a premature death as long as they kept the covenant. No babies, no young people, no middle-aged people died. With sickness taken away from the midst of them, they lived their lives out without disease, and then they just fell asleep in death. When it was time for them to go, they would lay hands on their children, pronounce blessings upon them, gather their feet up into bed, give up the ghost, and go home.

What does that have to do with us? God is the same God now that He was then! The Bible says that he does not change. God was against sin in the Old Testament (Old Covenant), and God is against sin in the New Testament (New Covenant). God was against sickness in the Old Testament — and God is against sickness in the New Testament. God made provision for healing in the Old Testament — and God has made provision for healing in the New Testament!

Confession: *I love and serve the Lord my God as a New Covenant believer. Jesus has taken sickness away from the midst of me. If He tarries His coming, the number of my days I will fulfill!*

With Long Life

The days of our years are threescore years and ten; and if by reason of strength they be fourscore years....
— PSALM 90:10

With long life will I satisfy him, and shew him my salvation.
— PSALM 91:16

If Jesus tarries His coming, I don't mind telling you at all, I'll live to a great age. And I'll know before I go. I will tell everybody good-bye and before I leave here, I'll look over there and say, "There it is, folks — and I'm going. I want to leave you all shouting and happy, because that's the way I'm going."

"But, Brother Hagin, you can't ever tell."

Oh yes, you can tell! You can have what God said you can have. We've got a better covenant than Israel had. If it was God's plan for Israel — who were servants, not sons, and who lived under a covenant not as good as ours — to live out their full length of time with no sickness, then what a plan God must have for us, the sons of God! If God didn't want His *servants* sick, I don't believe He wants His *sons* sick!

I believe it is the plan of God our Father that no believer should ever be sick, and that every believer should live his full length of time and actually wear out, if Jesus tarries, and fall asleep in Jesus.

Confession: *I can believe God for anything His Word promises. I can believe God for a long, productive life. If Jesus tarries, I will live out my days in His service without sickness and disease!*

80

For My Benefit

And he will love thee, and bless thee, and multiply thee: he will also bless the fruit of thy womb, and the fruit of thy land, thy corn, and thy wine, and thine oil, the increase of thy kine, and the flocks of thy sheep, in the land which he sware unto thy fathers to give thee. Thou shalt be blessed above all people: there shall not be male or female barren among you, or among your cattle. And the Lord will take away from thee all sickness, and will put [permit] none of the evil diseases of Egypt, which thou knowest, upon thee....

— DEUTERONOMY 7:13-15

"*And he will love thee....* " Love thee! Love thee!

And put sickness upon you? And cause you to die when you're a baby? And cause some of you to be stillborn, and some of you to be sick and crippled?

No! No! No! That's not the Holy Scriptures!

"But that's not for us today, Brother Hagin."

Are you sure? First Corinthians is in the New Testament, isn't it? Let's look at First Corinthians 10:11 to see if divine health is for us: "*Now all these things happened unto them* [Israel] *for ensamples* [examples, types]: *and they are written* [Who are they written for — the Jews? No!] *for OUR admonition, upon whom the ends of the world are come.*"

Glory! Deuteronomy 7:13-15 was written for my benefit. It was written for my admonition!

Confession: *Make your own confession of Deuteronomy 7:13-15. The Lord loves me ... He blesses me ... He blesses my children ... (and so on).*

Joint-Heirs

*The Spirit itself beareth witness with our spirit, that we
are the children of God: And if children, then heirs; heirs
of God, and joint-heirs with Christ....*

— ROMANS 8:16,17

Do you think the people who lived under the
Old Covenant could be more blessed than those
in the Church of the Lord Jesus Christ?

Do you think the people who lived under the
Old Covenant could be blessed financially, and be
well and healed, but those in the Church couldn't?

Do you think that the Church, the Body of
Christ, the Body of the Son of God, the Body of
the Beloved, would have to struggle through life
poverty-stricken, emaciated, wasted away with
starvation, sick and afflicted, singing, "Here I
wander, like a beggar, through the heat and the
cold"?

Away with such ideas!

The Bible declares that we are joint-heirs with
Christ! Sons of God! Children of God! In the
kingdom of God!

We're not beggars! We're new creatures.

We're blessed above all people.

Confession: *The Holy Spirit Himself bears witness with my
spirit that I am a child of God. God is my very own Father.
I am His very own child. And since I am His child, then
I am His heir. I am an heir of God, the Creator of the
universe, and I am a joint-heir with Jesus Christ!*

God's Stamp

He brought them forth also with silver and gold: and there was not one feeble person among their tribes.

— PSALM 105:37

You can see from the Scriptures that it was God's plan for everything connected with Israel to bear the stamp of prosperity and success. Furthermore, disease and sickness were not to be tolerated among them.

And so it should be with the Church. Everything connected with the Body of Christ, the New Testament Church, should bear the stamp of prosperity, success, healing, surplus, and health.

What God said concerning Israel, He said in so many words concerning the Church. Romans 1:16 says, *"For I am not ashamed of the gospel of Christ: for it is the power of God unto salvation. . . . "* Scofield's footnote on the word "salvation" states that the Greek and Hebrew words translated "salvation" imply the ideas of deliverance, safety, preservation, healing, and health (soundness). The Gospel of Jesus Christ, then, is the power of God unto deliverance. It is the power of God unto safety and preservation. It is the power of God unto healing and health.

Confession: *I am a child of God. I am a member of the Body of Christ. I bear the stamp of prosperity, success, healing, surplus, and health. The Gospel of Jesus Christ is the power of God unto deliverance, safety, preservation, healing, and health for me.*

Forgiveness and Healing

Who forgiveth all thine iniquities; who healeth all thy diseases.

— PSALM 103:3

Disease came upon the children of Israel when they disobeyed the law. Forgiveness for their disobedience meant the healing of their diseases.

It was when the children of Israel took themselves out from under the protection of their covenant by wrongdoing that their distresses came (Ps. 107:11,17,18). But when they cried unto the Lord, "... *he saveth them out of their distresses. He sent his word, and healed them, and delivered them from their destructions*" (Ps. 107:19,20).

We have protection under our better covenant — but it is possible to take ourselves out from under the protection of our covenant.

Since I have known the truth of God's Word concerning divine health and healing, the only time some physical disorder touched me was when I got out from under the protection. Now, I don't mean I stole something, or told a lie; I just wasn't obeying God like I should have been. (Usually, I wasn't ministering the way God said to minister.) And I got out from under the protection of the covenant and opened myself up to the enemy's attacks. So I had to repent and get back in line. The moment I did, I was healed physically.

Confession: *God forgives iniquities. God heals diseases. He sent His Word and healed me. He delivered me from destruction.*

Only Our Diseases

He was despised and shunned by men; a man of pains, and acquainted with disease; and as one who hid his face from us was he despised, and we esteemed him not. But only our diseases did he bear himself, and our pains he carried: while we indeed esteemed him stricken, smitten of God, and afflicted. Yet he was wounded for our transgressions, he was bruised for our iniquities: the chastisement for our peace was upon him; and through his bruises was healing granted to us.

— ISAIAH 53:3-5 *Leeser*, Hebrew Publishing Co.

I want to boldly state that it is not the will of God my Father that we should suffer from cancer and other dread diseases that bring pain and anguish. It is God's will that we be healed!

How do I know? Because healing is provided for us under the New Covenant.

The fifty-third chapter of Isaiah gives us a graphic picture of the coming Messiah. This chapter deals with the disease problem which confronts the Church today, as well as the sin problem.

God dealt with man's body, as well as with his spirit and soul. God laid our iniquities and our sins upon Jesus — and Jesus bore them. God laid our diseases and our sicknesses on Jesus — and Jesus bore them. Why? So that we might be free!

Confession: *Jesus Christ, the Lamb of God, bore my sins and iniquities. So I don't have to bear them. He also bore my diseases and pains. So I don't have to bear them. Because of Jesus, I am free. By His stripes, I was healed!*

Himself Took . . . And Bare

That it might be fulfilled which was spoken by Esaias the prophet, saying, Himself took our infirmities, and bare our sicknesses.

— MATTHEW 8:17

In our text today, Matthew is quoting Isaiah 53.

When I first understood what this verse really meant, I rejoiced in it. Because when I read it, I was able to emphasize the word "our." Jesus took *our* infirmities and bore *our* sicknesses. I am included in that *our!* He took *my* infirmities, and bore *my* sicknesses!

At this realization I felt as the elderly woman did who suddenly turned up missing in London during World War II. Her neighbors didn't see her in the bomb shelters during enemy air raids, so they assumed she had either been killed or had left town. When some of them saw her on the street several days later, they asked where she had been. She answered that she hadn't been anywhere.

"But what did you do during the bombing?"

"I just stayed in bed and slept."

"Weren't you afraid?"

"No, after I read in the Bible that God neither slumbers nor sleeps, I decided there wasn't any need for both of us to stay awake!"

Since Christ Himself took our infirmities and bore our sicknesses, there isn't any need for us to bear them. Jesus bore them so that we might be free!

Confession: *Because Christ took my infirmities and bore my sicknesses, there is no need for me to bear them. I accept what Jesus has provided!*

By His Stripes

Who his own self bare our sins in his own body on the tree,
that we, being dead to sins, should live unto righteousness:
by whose stripes ye were healed.

— 1 PETER 2:24

Some years ago, I was awakened at 1:30 a.m. with severe symptoms in my heart and chest. I knew something about such symptoms, because I had been bedfast and given up to die with a heart condition as a teenager.

The devil said to my mind, "You're going to die. This is one time you're *not* going to get your healing."

I pulled the covers over my head and began to laugh. I didn't feel like laughing, but I just laughed anyway for about ten minutes. Finally, the devil asked me what I was laughing about.

"I'm laughing at you!" I said, "You said I wasn't going to get my healing. Ha, ha, Mr. Devil. I don't *expect* to get my healing! Jesus already *got* it for me! Now, in case you can't read, I'll quote First Peter 2:24 for you." And I did.

After quoting the last phrase, "*. . . by whose stripes ye were healed,*" I said, "Now, if we *were* — I *was!* So I don't have to get it — Jesus already got it! And because Jesus got it for me, I accept it, and claim it, and I have it. Now you just gather up your little symptoms and get out of here, Mr. Devil!"

And he did!

Confession: *Jesus has already obtained healing for me. I accept it. I claim it. I have it. By Jesus' stripes I was healed!*

Travel Safety

And the same day, when the even was come, he saith unto them, Let us pass over unto the other side.

— MARK 4:35

Jesus got into a ship with His disciples and said, "Let us pass over unto the other side." And that settled it! Jesus did not say, "Let us go halfway and sink." Therefore, when a storm arose and Jesus' disciples were frightened, He rebuked them, saying, "How is it that you have no faith?"

At a Full Gospel Business Men's convention, a woman came to me and asked me to pray for her. She said, "I'm a nervous wreck. It just scares me to death to travel by plane. I actually become sick with fright. I'm not going to attend any more conventions, even though I love to, because I'm too afraid to fly."

"You don't have to be afraid," I replied. "And really, you don't even have to pray about it. All you have to do is get on the plane and say, 'Let us pass over to Los Angeles, or Chicago, or wherever.' And the plane can't go down. Then you can do just what Jesus did: You can go to sleep, knowing the plane is going to get there because you have spoken in faith."

I saw this woman at several conventions afterwards. She told me, "It works just like you said. I get on board the plane and say, 'Let's go over to the other side.' Then I lie back, relax, and praise the Lord. I'm really enjoying flying now."

Confession: *Wherever I travel, I can say, "Let us pass over to the other side"* — *and I will have what I say!*

No Accident

The angel of the Lord encampeth round about them that fear him, and delivereth them.

— PSALM 34:7

In May 1952, my wife and children were traveling with me to a tent meeting in New Mexico. When my mother learned of our travel plans, she said, "Be careful on the road! There are so many wrecks. When you're traveling, I stay awake all night praying for your safety, and just waiting for the phone to ring with the news that you've been in a wreck. But I know that you're praying that Jesus will be with you every minute you're on that road."

"I never do," I replied.

"Oh, Son, what's gotten into you?"

"Nothing but the Word," I said. "Jesus has already said, ' . . . *I will never leave thee, nor forsake thee*' (Heb. 13:5). So I don't have to go down the road begging Jesus to be with me. I always start out by saying, 'Heavenly Father, I'm so thankful for your Word. I'm so glad Jesus is with me. I'm so glad the Father, Son, and Holy Spirit are inside me.' Then I go singing and rejoicing. God has already told me in Psalm 91 that no evil will overtake me. And the Swedish translation of that reads, 'No accident shall overtake thee.' "

Confession: *Jesus never leaves me. Angels are encamped around about me. The Father, the Son, and the Holy Spirit live inside of me. No accident can overtake me!*

The Law of Life

For the law of the Spirit of life in Christ Jesus hath made me free from the law of sin and death.

— ROMANS 8:2

Dr. John G. Lake went as a missionary to Africa in 1908. The deadly bubonic plague broke out in his area. Hundreds died. He cared for the sick and buried the dead. Finally the British sent a relief ship with medical supplies and a corps of doctors. The doctors sent for Lake to come aboard. They asked him, "What have you been using to protect yourself?"

"Sirs," Lake replied, "I believe the law of the Spirit of life in Christ Jesus has set me free from the law of sin and death. And as long as I walk in the light of that law of life, no germ will attach itself to me."

"You had better use our preventatives," the doctors urged.

"No," Lake said, "but I think you would like to experiment with me. Take some of the foam that comes from the victims' lungs after death and examine it under a microscope. You will find the masses of living germs remain alive for a while after a man is dead. Fill my hand with the foam and examine it under the microscope. Instead of remaining alive, the germs will die instantly."

The doctors made the experiment and what Lake said proved true. When the doctors expressed wonder at what caused it, Lake told them, "That is the law of the Spirit of life in Christ Jesus."

Confession: *The law of the Spirit of life in Christ Jesus has made me free from the law of sin and death.*

More Than Conquerors

Nay, in all these things we are more than conquerors through him that loved us.

— ROMANS 8:37

If God's Word had just told us we were conquerors, it would have been enough — but it tells us that we are *more than conquerors* through Jesus Christ.

Rather than saying, "I'm defeated," rise up and say what the Bible says about you. Say, "I am a conqueror!"

It may not seem to you that you are a conqueror, but your confession of it because of what you see in God's Word will create the reality of it in your life.

Sooner or later you will become what you confess!

You will not be afraid of any circumstances, if you make the right confession.

You will not be afraid of any disease, if you make the right confession.

You will not be afraid of any conditions, if you make the right confession.

You will face life fearlessly, as a conqueror!

Confession: *In all things I am more than a conqueror through Him that loves me. I am not afraid of any circumstances. I am not afraid of any disease. I am not afraid of any condition. I face life fearlessly, a conqueror! I am a conqueror! In fact, I am more than a conqueror!*

Working in Me

For it is God which worketh in you both to will and to do of his good pleasure.

— PHILIPPIANS 2:13

Another translation of this verse reads, "For it is God who is at work within you. . . ."

I like to put Philippians 2:13 together with First John 4:4: ". . . *greater is he that is in you* [and that means me]. . . ." God is in me!

What is God doing in me?

He is at work in me.

What is God working at?

Both to will and to do of His own good pleasure.

What is His own good pleasure?

His pleasure is that I have everything the Word of God says I can have — that I do everything the Word of God says I can do. God is enabling me!

God is in there, and my spirit rejoices. My heart is glad that I can turn God loose in me. I can let God have right-of-way in me. I can put God to work even to a greater degree in my life.

How can I do this?

First, I can do it by believing in my heart that God is in there, and that the Word of God is true. Then, I can boldly confess with my mouth. For I will not enjoy the reality of what the Word states is mine or what I believe until I confess it with my mouth. The Bible teaches that " . . . *with the heart man believeth . . . and with the mouth confession is made unto. . . .*"

Confession: *God is in me. God is at work within me. God works through me!*